Leading Every Day

Leading Every Day

124 Actions for Effective Leadership

Joyce Kaser
Susan Mundry
Katherine E. Stiles
Susan Loucks-Horsley

CORWIN PRESS, INC.
A Sage Publications Company
Thousand Oaks, California

This book is a product of WestEd's National Academy for Sciences and Mathematics Educational Leadership. The Academy is supported by the National Science Foundation under Contract #9619007. Any opinions, findings, and conclusions or recommendations expressed in this publication are those of the authors and do not necessarily reflect the view of the National Science Foundation.

For information:

Corwin Press, Inc.
A Sage Publications Company
2455 Teller Road
Thousand Oaks, California 91320
E-mail: order@corwinpress.com

Sage Publications Ltd.
6 Bonhill Street
London EC2A 4PU
United Kingdom

Sage Publications India Pvt. Ltd.
M-32 Market
Greater Kailash I
New Delhi 110 048 India

Printed in the United States of America

Library of Congress Cataloging-in-Publication Data

Leading every day: 124 actions for effective leadership / by Joyce Kaser ... [et al.].
    p. cm.
  Includes bibliographical references and index.
  ISBN 0-7619-4512-1 (cloth)—ISBN 0-7619-4513-X (pbk.)
  1. Educational leadership—Handbooks, manuals, etc. 2. School management and organization—Handbooks, manuals, etc. I. Kaser, Joyce S.
  LB2805 .L345 2002
  371.2—dc21   2001004506

This book is printed on acid-free paper.

01 02 03 04 05 06 07 7 6 5 4 3 2 1

Acquisitions Editor:	Robb Clouse
Associate Editor:	Kylee Liegl
Editorial Assistant:	Erin Buchanan
Production Editor:	Diane S. Foster
Copy Editor:	Carla Freeman
Proofreader:	Jamie Robinson
Typesetter/Designer:	Larry K. Bramble
Cover Designer:	Michael Dubowe

▨ CONTENTS

Acknowledgments ix

About the Authors xi

Susan Loucks-Horsley:
A Tribute to Her Life and Work xv

About the National Academy
for Science and Mathematics
Education Leadership xvii

Introduction xix

BOOK ONE: Leadership Every Day 1

Day 1: Defining Leadership 2
Day 2: Making Choices 4
Day 3: Extraversion and Introversion 6
Day 4: Vision Building 8
Day 5: Leading and Managing 10
Day 6: Processing Information 11
Day 7: Managing Information 13
Day 8: Focusing on Customers 15
Day 9: Making Decisions 17
Day 10: Coping With Change 19
Day 11: Judging and Perceiving 21
Day 12: Networking 23
Day 13: Leading With Principles 24
Day 14: Leadership Styles 25
Day 15: Reframing Your Perspective 27
Day 16: Resolving Paradox 29
Day 17: Working Synergistically 30
Day 18: Balancing the Whole 32
Day 19: Sharing Vision 34
Day 20: Exploring Relationships 36
Day 21: Unity and Diversity 38
Day 22: Planning 40
Day 23: Breaking Static Patterns 42
Day 24: Positioning 44
Day 25: Transactional and Transformational Leadership 46
Day 26: Examining Your Beliefs 48
Day 27: Communicating 50

Day 28: Knowing Your Organizational Culture 52
Day 29: Problem Solving 54
Day 30: Choosing a Power Base 56
Day 31: Doing the Right Thing 58

BOOK TWO: Leading Change 61

Part I: Planning and Directing 62
Day 1: Change as Process 63
Day 2: Stages of Change 65
Day 3: Individual Change 67
Day 4: Using Data to Guide Change Efforts 69
Day 5: Planning for Change 71
Day 6: Change as Continuous Improvement 73
Day 7: Complexity of Change 75

Part II: Listening to Individuals 77
Day 8: Change as a People Process 78
Day 9: The Impact of Change 79
Day 10: Moving Through the Stages of Change 81
Day 11: Accepting Loss 83
Day 12: Change and Resilience 85
Day 13: Embracing Problems 87

Part III: Responsibilities in Directing Change 88
Day 14: Motivating Others 89
Day 15: Origins of Change 91
Day 16: Balancing Constants and Change 93
Day 17: Applying Personal Mastery 95
Day 18: Recognizing Mental Models 97
Day 19: Shared Vision 99
Day 20: Missions and Goals 101
Day 21: Tackling Resistance 103
Day 22: Establishing Stakeholder Information Systems 105
Day 23: Managing Multiple Change Efforts 107
Day 24: Capitalizing on Resistance 109
Day 25: Empowering Others 111
Day 26: Modeling Behavior 113
Day 27: Self-Assessment as a Change Leader 115

Part IV: Paying Attention to the Organization 117
Day 28: Systems Thinking 118
Day 29: Identifying Organizational Character 120
Day 30: Examining Change History 122
Day 31: Launching and Sustaining Change Initiatives 124

BOOK THREE: Leading Learning 127

Part I: A Framework for Planning   128
Day 1:   Designing Professional Development   129

Part II: Emerging Practices   132
Day 2:   Contemporary Professional Development   133
Day 3:   Lifelong Learning   135
Day 4:   Personal Mastery   137
Day 5:   Learning Organizations   139
Day 6:   Additive and Transformative Learning   141
Day 7:   Reflection and Cognitive Apprenticeships   143
Day 8:   Aligning Assumptions and Behaviors   145

Part III: Context and Strategies   147
Day 9:   Contextual Professional Development   148
Day 10: Strategies for Professional Networks   150
Day 11: Situational Strategies   153
Day 12: Professional Networks   155
Day 13: Action Research   157

Part IV: Designing Learning Experiences   159
Day 14: Examining Learning Styles   160
Day 15: Powerful Learning Experiences   162
Day 16: Balancing Philosophy and Pragmatism   164
Day 17: Thinking to Learn Versus Learning to Think   166
Day 18: Incorporating Reflexive Practice   168
Day 19: Equity and Diversity   170
Day 20: Reaching Everyone, or Scaling Up   173
Day 21: Twelve Principles of Knowledge Acquisition   175
Day 22: Transferring Situational Learning   177

Part V: Teams Learning Together   179
Day 23: Team Learning   180
Day 24: Matching Interventions With Desired Outcomes   182

Part VI: Evaluating Professional Development   184
Day 25: Achieving Desired Outcomes   185
Day 26: Gathering Evaluation Data   187
Day 27: Identifying Key Features of Successful Programs   189
Day 28: Capturing Lessons Learned   191

Part VII: Modeling Expertise   193
Day 29: Defining Expertise   194
Day 30: Modeling Lifelong Learning   196
Day 31: Ten-Step Plan for Lifelong Learning   198

BOOK FOUR: Leading Effective Groups   202

Part I: Developing a Community Environment   203
Day 1: Four Roles of Group Leaders   204
Day 2: Group Norms of Collaboration   206
Day 3: Group Norm #1—Pausing   208
Day 4: Group Norm #2—Paraphrasing   211
Day 5: Group Norm #3—Probing   213
Day 6: Group Norm #4—Putting Ideas on the Table
        or Pulling Them Off   215
Day 7: Group Norm #5—Paying Attention to Self and Others,
        Verbal Communication   217
Day 8: Group Norm #5—Paying Attention to
        Self and Others, Nonverbal Communication   219
Day 9: Group Norm #6—Presuming Positive Intentions   221
Day 10: Group Norm #7—Pursuing a Balance Between
        Advocacy and Inquiry   223
Day 11: Dialogue Versus Discussion   225
Day 12: Dialogue as Reflective Learning Process   228

Part II: Key Aspects of Effective Group Functioning   230
Day 13: Sources of Group Energy   231
Day 14: Establishing Clear Roles and Functions   234
Day 15: Structuring an Effective Meeting   238
Day 16: Providing Logistical Supports   240
Day 17: Setting Up the Meeting Room   242
Day 18: Group Decision Making   244
Day 19: Reaching Consensus   246
Day 20: Dealing With Conflict   248
Day 21: Conflict as Opportunity   250
Day 22: Don't Shoot the Messenger   252
Day 23: Resolving Conflict   255
Day 24: Impact of Bias and Stereotyping   257
Day 25: Dealing With Disruptive People   260
Day 26: Eliciting Participation From Everyone   262
Day 27: Giving Negative Feedback   264
Day 28: Receiving Negative Feedback   266
Day 29: Presentation Skills   268
Day 30: Handling Problems   271
Day 31: Six Domains of Group Development   273

▧ Acknowledgments

Translating the curriculum of the National Academy for Science and Mathematics Education Leadership into the 124 contemplations in this book was not a solitary task. Our deep appreciation goes to our WestEd colleague Kathy DiRanna, whose spirit and enthusiasm for the Leadership Academy and for this book has continued to energize us. Our special thanks go to the academy fellows, mentors, and advisors who reviewed the book and offered valuable suggestions and insights. For this we thank Richard Audet, Susan Brady, Karen Falkenberg, Kelly Jacobs, Page Keeley, Nancy Kellogg, Paul Kuerbis, Emma Walton, and Sybil Yastrow. We thank Kendall Zoller who, in addition to his review of the manuscript, wrote material for the group facilitation chapter. Our special thanks go to our many colleagues who contributed heartfelt tributes to Susan Loucks-Horsley's memory. Friends and colleagues of the authors who provided input and background information include: Stan Altrock, Terry Brill, Nancy Love, Marilyn Lutz, Norm Mitchell, Judith Noel, Ronald Richmond, Marlene Ross, and Robert Terry. We thank each of you for your assistance.

Our special thanks goes to Deanna Maier of the Leadership Academy staff, who prepared the final manuscript and made numerous helpful suggestions. We appreciate your hard work and dedication. Thanks also go to Diane Enright, who once again helped us finish a quality manuscript under tight deadlines.

Finally, we thank all of the fellows, mentors, and advisors of the leadership academy who have taught us so much about leadership development. Thank you for sharing your enthusiasm, insights, and experiences. The learning community we have established will nurture us all for many years to come.

◪ About the Authors

Joyce S. Kaser (EdD, American University, Washington, D.C.), is a Senior Program Associate with WestEd. She is also President of Kaser and Associates and is a Senior Research Associate with The Study Group. She is first author of *Enhancing Program Quality in Science and Mathematics,* also published by Corwin Press, in 1999. This book presents an approach, called *profiling,* to formative evaluation of programs that support mathematics and science education. Over the past decade, Dr. Kaser has been one of the key developers of this methodology. She has also been an evaluator of state, urban, and local systemic change efforts, along with numerous national and statewide professional development programs. Currently, she is part of a team developing statewide criteria for professional development and serves as the coprincipal investigator of research for an online learning program. She assists a major professional development provider implement profiling as its approach to quality assurance. A former teacher and school administrator, Dr. Kaser is coauthor of a change management methodology for use in education, along with a risk analysis assessment process for large system interventions. This new book brings together her work in professional development, evaluation, change management, lifelong learning, and group leadership.

Susan Mundry is a Project Director at WestEd, where she leads the National Academy of Science and Mathematics Education Leadership, a leadership development program for leaders of systemic reform. She designs and conducts leadership development on the roles of new leaders, organizational change, effective adult development, and group facilitation. She also conducts research and develops educational products on professional development. She is the coprincipal investigator and lead writer for the Teachers as Learners Project, which is developing a set of videotapes, a guidebook, and Web site activities. They will illustrate diverse strategies for teacher learning drawn from successful programs in operation across the country.

Susan is also the author of *Designing Successful Professional Meetings and Conferences in Education, Planning, Implementation, and Evaluation* (2000) and *Global Perspectives for Local Action Professional Development Guide: Using TIMSS to Improve U.S. Mathematics and Science Education* (1999). She is codeveloper of the "Change Games," two acclaimed simulation board games on organizational change: *Making Change for School Improvement* and *Systems Thinking/Systems Changing.*

In addition to her duties at WestEd, Susan is also a partner in ST&C Associates, a business she cofounded in 1997 to help organizations use systems thinking and other effective processes to become learning organizations. Prior to this, she was Associate Director at THE NETWORK, Inc., an educational consulting organization focused on organizational change and dissemination of innovative practice.

Katherine E. Stiles is a Project Director and Research Associate at WestEd, where she leads projects focused on professional development, leadership development, and evaluation in science education. She is the lead evaluator for the NSF-funded Local Systemic Change initiative, the DESERT Project, in the Tucson (AZ) Unified School District, which supports science education reform in the district through teacher professional development. She is Codirector of WestEd's National Academy for Science and Mathematics Education Leadership, designed to enhance the knowledge, skills, and strategies of current leaders of science and mathematics education reform. She also works with science and mathematics education leaders in designing and implementing "replication" models of the Leadership Academy in their own states.

Her work with the National Institute for Science Education (NISE) to examine models of effective professional development for mathematics and science teachers resulted in coauthorship of the book *Designing Professional Development for Teachers of Science and Mathematics.* She works as a consultant in helping district and state leaders design and implement leadership development programs and professional development programs. She also designs and conducts program evaluation for science education projects.

Prior to her work at WestEd, Katherine was a curriculum development specialist at the National Science Resources Center in Washington, D.C., where she developed and wrote elementary science units for the Science and Technology for Children project. She also worked as the K-12 Professional Development Specialist at the National Academy of Science Center for Science, Mathematics, and Engineering Education. There, she coordinated the dissemination efforts of the *National Science Education Standards Project* and designed and implemented the 1999 State Leadership Institute for over 70 state science and mathematics supervisors.

Susan Loucks-Horsley was Associate Executive Director at Biological Sciences Curriculum Study (BSCS) and Senior Research Associate for Science and Mathematics at WestEd. She directed the Professional Development Project at the National Institute for Science Education and was senior author of the project's *Designing Professional Development for Teachers of Science and Mathematics*, published in 1998. Previously, she was the Director of Professional Development and Outreach at the National Research Council (NRC) Center for Science, Mathematics, and Engineering Education. Her work at the NRC included promoting, supporting, and monitoring the progress of standards-based education, especially the *National Science Education Standards*. Her work as Associate Director of the Northeast/Islands Regional Lab and the National Center for Improving Science Education focused on developing approaches, products, and training activities to help educators build their knowledge and skills in collaborative approaches to staff development, program change, and program evaluation. She led the development team of *Facilitating Systemic Change in Science and Mathematics Education: A Toolkit for Professional Developers*, a product of the 10 regional education laboratories. She was senior author of *Continuing to Learn: A Guidebook for Teacher Development, An Action Guide for School Improvement, Elementary School Science for the '90s*, reports from the National Center for Improving Science Education on teacher development and support, and numerous chapters and articles on related topics. While at the University of Texas (Austin) Research and Development Center for Teacher Education, she worked on the development team of the Concerns-Based Adoption Model (CBAM), which describes how individuals experience change.

▧ Susan Loucks-Horsley

A Tribute to Her Life and Work, 1947–2000

This book is dedicated to our coauthor and dear friend, Susan Loucks-Horsley, whose visionary leadership and tireless dedication to education reform inspired so many.

The National Academy for Science and Mathematics Education Leadership (on which this book is based) was a dream realized for Susan. For many years, she had talked with colleagues about the need to build the next generation of leaders for education. She had a vision of a leadership academy that would be a national network, in which leaders learned from and supported each other. The academy she developed and directed, like Susan's many other endeavors, was a tremendous success. Through this and other achievements, she carried out the work she cared so passionately about—the continual improvement of education for children and professional development opportunities for educators.

Susan was loved and admired by so many people. Upon her death, we received hundreds of e-mails and notes from people whose lives had been touched by her. People conveyed how she had inspired them to think and act differently, to take on new roles, and to support others to get greater results. Here are just a few of the thoughtful words our colleagues and friends shared with us:

- Susan lived the words of Teilhard de Chardin: "*We are not human beings on a spiritual journey. We are spiritual beings on a human journey.*" Namaste, Susan. We honor the divinity in you.

- I expect that Susan Loucks-Horsley's educational leadership will transcend generations.

- Susan helped us create an awareness of our own individual and collective potential as professional developers.

- Disraeli said that the mark of a truly great person was not just someone who gave gifts, but someone who brought out the gifts in others. This was Susan's special gift.

- Not only did Susan give me tremendous ideas about serving teachers and students in the nation's third largest school district, she was able to take off some of my "rough edges" and to teach me the importance of a smile and a kind word. She is one of my personal heroes.

- Susan had the wonderful ability to help me gain deeper insights into my own understandings as well as introduce me to hers.

- Susan created the forks in the road, pointed you in that direction, and helped forge the new road "less traveled"—and that has made all the difference.

- Susan continually sought ways to connect people to one another and to ideas, often doing so behind the scenes and always without desire for acknowledgement or recognition.

- Susan was one of those rare individuals who by following her heart has touched the lives of thousands of children.

- Susan, through her work, convinced me to stay in the field of education, and I will spend the rest of my life trying to make a difference.

- Susan has touched the lives of so many children across the nation through professional development to the leaders and teachers. I am blessed to be one of those leaders.

- Susan's wisdom, knowledge and friendship drew all of us toward her. Our memories will keep a part of her with us, and her work will continue to touch others.

- Susan, though you are no longer with us in person, your spirit will remain forever in us: in our hearts, our memories and our work. Continue to guide us from afar so we can remain true to your dreams and ours.

- Susan, you will always live on in just the way you hoped to—in the hearts, the hard work, the tireless efforts, and the memories of those of us who admired, respected, and loved you dearly.

Susan will live on in the work and hearts of the many people she shared herself with so generously during her remarkable career. We give tribute to her and promise to carry on her vision and passion for leadership development. Susan's middle name was Hope, and she had it in abundance. Our hope is that her work lives on in you as you take up and use the ideas and reflections on leadership, change, learning, and group facilitation in this book.

—Joyce S. Kaser, Susan Mundry, and Katherine E. Stiles

◪ About the National Academy for Science and Mathematics Education Leadership

The Leadership Academy is an in-depth professional development experience for leaders of science and mathematics education reform. The Leadership Academy's curriculum focuses on leadership styles and models, organizational change, strategic planning and organizational development, facilitation skills, and professional development design and evaluation. These topics are explored in the context of six major issues related to standards-based science and mathematics education reform:

- Developing, revising, or implementing standards and frameworks
- Equity
- Public support
- Assessment
- Content and curriculum
- Instructional strategies

This project is a collaboration between WestEd—a research, development, and service agency working with education and other communities to promote excellence, achieve equity, and improve learning for children, youth, and adults—and the organizations listed below. It supported three cohorts of leaders and was funded by the National Science Foundation.

- Association for the Education of Teachers in Science (AETS)
- Association for State Supervisors of Mathematics (ASSM)
- Council of State Science Supervisors (CSSS)
- National Council of Supervisors of Mathematics (NCSM)
- National Staff Development Council (NSDC)
- National Science Education Leadership Association (NSELA)
- National Science Teachers Association (NSTA)
- National Research Council, Center for Science, Mathematics, and Engineering Education (CSMEE)

For additional information about the Leadership Academy, contact WestEd's Tucson Office: 4732 North Oracle Road, Suite 217, Tucson, AZ 85705. Telephone: (520) 888-2838. Fax: (520) 888-2621.

▨ Introduction

This book provides leaders—and those who aspire to be leaders—with information in four areas to help them lead reform efforts in their schools, districts, or other organizations. These areas are leadership, change management, lifelong learning, and group facilitation. Although the primary audience is made up of leaders in science and mathematics reform, the content is applicable to others who may be leading major transitions in their organizations.

There are four books: Leadership Every Day, Leading Change, Leading Learning, and Leading Effective Groups. For each book, the material is presented in 31 contemplations, one for each day of the month. Each contemplation begins with a quote, presents some aspect of the topic, and ends with a reflection, usually a series of questions or a scenario for the reader to consider.

We recommend that a reader go through the contemplations in order during the first reading. After that, he or she may turn to a section at random to find a particular contemplation. The contemplations are best read in an environment that is conducive to reflection, when the reader has time to consider the questions and write thoughtful responses.

Most of the material in this book was part of the curriculum of the National Academy for Science and Mathematics Education Leadership. Participants in the Leadership Academy were responsible for leading science and mathematics education reform. The material in the leadership academy provided them with the knowledge and perspectives to carry out this role. We believe that the material is useful for all persons responsible for leading change efforts in any type of organization: local, regional, state, or national—public or private.

In the spirit of continuous learning, we hope that the contemplations help leaders to reflect often on their leadership roles, styles, and practices. We believe the insights leaders gain will sustain them through challenging transitions.

Book One

▨ Leadership Every Day

This first book is a collection of thoughts and inspirations on the topic of leadership. The authors envision a time when many, rather than a few, people are leading creatively every day and in all aspects of their lives. Today's world cries out for such leadership in schools, communities, and the workplace.

The contemplations address many of the basic questions about leaders and leadership. Who are leaders? What makes leaders leaders? What is leadership? What do leaders do? What types of power do they use? How do they set in place a shared vision and mission? How do leaders use group synergy, manage paradoxes, reframe problems, and clarify roles and responsibilities? What is their leadership style? How can leaders use their strengths while compensating for their weaknesses, considering that no leader does everything with the same high degree of proficiency?

Another important question is this: What is likely to trip up leaders? Is it inability to cope with change, inflexibility, lack of skill in bringing about win/win agreements, or making erroneous assumptions? How can leaders maneuver around or remove these obstacles? How do leaders establish the type of environment that supports excellent leadership? How do they communicate, and how do they know what messages they send to others? And finally, how do leaders know that they're doing the right thing? These topics are interwoven through the Day 1–31 contemplations.

▨ DAY 1: Defining Leadership

The leadership we need is available in all of us.
We have only to make it manifest.

—Harrison Owen

Are you a leader?

Have you wrestled with this question maybe once or twice in your career, or maybe more frequently?

Perhaps part of the reason for your persistent question is that definitions abound, each reflecting one of the different theories of leadership. According to some, you may be a leader; according to others, you are not.

One common definition of leadership is an individual's ability to work with others to accomplish some agreed-upon end.

Note that what *isn't* in this definition is as important as what *is*. It says absolutely nothing about position, title, or status. Sometimes, having the right job or an impressive title helps—but not always. The ability to influence (i.e., to use personal power positively) is what underlies leadership, regardless of how much institutional power you may have.

Also, leadership is much less an ongoing role than it is action taken in the moment. Everyone has the capacity for leadership. On any given day, the extent to which you might act on that capacity varies.

The focus of personal power is working with others. One of the authors recalls a time when her daughter was in a difficult situation at school. She specifically asked her mother not to come to talk with the principal or her teachers. When asked why, she replied, "Every time you come to school, Mom, something happens." She was referring to her mother's ability to influence others, to some end, to resolve a problem. Now that she was older, the child wanted to handle the situation herself—to try her hand at influencing others rather than having her mother intervene.

▨ Reflection

The greater your ability to influence and mobilize others, the greater your capacity for leadership. Here are some questions that assess your ability to influence others. When you are in a given situation, do you . . .

- Have a clear vision of what you want?
- Model the behavior you want to see in others?
- Empower others to be more powerful themselves?
- Act ethically?
- Rely on positional power less than your ability to influence others?

What are your strengths? What needs improvement?

▨ Notes

_____

_____

_____

_____

_____

_____

_____

_____

_____

_____

_____

_____

_____

▨ DAY 2: Making Choices

This inherent capacity to choose, to develop a new vision for ourselves, to rescript our life, to begin a new habit or let go of an old one, to forgive someone, to apologize, to make a promise and then keep it, in any area of life, is, always has been, and always will be a moment of truth for every true leader.

—Stephen Covey

Choose. Choose often—hundreds of times a day, in fact.

Choose. Choose based on what you desire—what you truly want for yourself and others.

Choose. Choose deliberately and consciously. Choose, if you want to move forward. Don't choose, and you stay stationary or fall back.

One of the key characteristics of leaders is that they consciously make all kinds of choices—not just the big ones, such as instituting new policies or launching mergers. They make medium-sized choices, such as choosing not to blame themselves for failure or be deterred from their mission by adversaries. They also make many small choices: choosing to ask a colleague about an ill child or picking up dirty coffee cups at the end of a meeting. And each of the choices leaders make says something about what they stand for and what they want for themselves and their organizations.

As a leader of change efforts in your organization, there are two arenas in which making choices is critical:

Choose to know what you want. Oftentimes, we don't proceed because we don't know what we want. Although it is not easy, you can develop a conscious habit of knowing what you want. It may be a meeting with an influential person in your organization, having a pleasant exchange with an obstreperous colleague, or having a cup of tea instead of coffee. Think of yourself as always having an answer to the question, if it were posed, "What is it that you want right now? Five days from now? Five years from now?"

Choose to act to achieve what you want. Perhaps all you have to do to get the meeting you want is to call and ask. People often don't get what they want because they never make their wishes known. They just keep them to themselves. The sheer act of asking will accomplish a great deal. Perhaps to achieve what you want, you must take a next step: Set a meeting date, write a position paper, or recommend a new program. Each day, try to take at least one step that moves you toward your goals.

▨ Reflection

During the day, stop periodically to ask yourself what choices you are making and why. If you want something at that moment, what is it? Take an extra minute or two for yourself if you don't readily have an answer to that question. Chances are that you do want something—maybe five minutes to call home or to sign a contract for your next professional development activity. Once you find what it is, choose it for yourself. At the end of the day, tally what you gained for yourself and your organization by making conscious, deliberate choices.

Look over your list. How many of the items relate directly to what you are trying to accomplish? How can you do more of these things and less of the things that may not affect your goals?

▨ Notes

_____

_____

_____

_____

_____

_____

_____

_____

_____

▨ DAY 3: Extraversion and Introversion

How do you converse? Do you talk to think or think to talk?

—Joyce S. Kaser

Where do you derive your energy?

Are you energized by the external world of people, events, and things and drained by being left to your own devices? Or are you energized by your own internal world of thoughts and reflections and exhausted by having to interact with the external world?

If you gain energy from the external, chances are, you interact freely with others, have a broad range of interests, have a large circle of friends, are gregarious in nature, and are transparent in the sense that you let people know where you stand.

If you generate your own energy internally, chances are, you are more guarded in your interactions with others unless you know and trust them, you have great depth in a limited number of areas, have a small circle of friends, are more quiet and reflective in nature, and often keep your true thoughts and feelings to yourself.

These descriptions characterize two basic aspects of personality, according to Carl Jung (1921/1971) and Isabel Briggs Myers (Myers, McCaulley, Quenk, & Hammer, 1998): extraversion and introversion. Note that the definitions here focus on the source of energy, a much different case than in dictionary definitions or common usage of these two terms.

People preferring either extraversion or introversion can be more influential in leading by keeping the following in mind:

If you prefer extraversion, watch how much "airtime" you take up. Try to think before you speak or take a moment to jot down and organize your ideas on paper before speaking out. Others in your group will tend to discount your contributions if you make too many of them or if you ramble on without making your point succinctly. Make sure that your questions and comments are targeted and timely.

If you prefer introversion, you need to speak up occasionally. You can't exert influence in a group unless you speak. Make sure that you have questions and comments and that they also are targeted and timely.

One of the authors was coaching the chief financial officer (CFO) of a municipality. The mayor reported that the CFO rarely contributed in meetings. Instead, he had a maddening habit of returning to his office after meetings and sending out long e-mail messages to the executive team with his thoughts about the meeting. This was especially frustrating because the group made decisions that it might not have made if the CFO had spoken up at the time. Through reflection, the group realized that it was dominated by extraverts. All information was shared verbally; opinions were offered on the spot. To compensate for this tendency, the group adjusted its meeting style. Members shared information in writing before the meeting and took short breaks prior to making decisions. This gave the CFO the time he needed to reflect on financial implications and to feel comfortable speaking up.

Although you have a preference for one over the other, to be an effective leader, you need to be able to think and act using your preference along with exercising some skills in your nonpreference. For example, if you prefer extraversion, can you work alone if necessary? If you claim introversion, can you work as a member of a large team? The primary goal of understanding your preference is self-management. A secondary goal is knowing others' preferences in order to better understand them and work with them effectively.

▨ Reflection

Do you know your preference? Can you use your nonpreference when the circumstances dictate that you do so? Are you sensitive to those who have preferences that are different from yours? Do you make judgments or assumptions about a person's competence and commitment based on how little or how much he or she speaks in a group? What factors could be contributing to a person's level of participation in a group?

▨ Notes

_____

_____

_____

_____

_____

_____

▨ DAY 4: Vision Building

The test of a vision is not in the statement, but in the directional force it gives the organization.
    —From *The Fifth Discipline Fieldbook*, Peter Senge et al.

Vision! What is your reaction to this word?

Is it negative? Perhaps you have been involved in vision-building activities that have turned out to be a waste of time. Perhaps your organization, like many others, failed to live by a vision once it was created.

True leaders engage people throughout the organization in building commitment toward a shared vision that is the guiding force for all action. Building a shared vision results in stronger commitment than a vision imposed exclusively from the top. At the same time, leaders must model and communicate the vision in all their actions. There are different ways to do this.

Usually, vision building is thinking into the future and determining where an organization wants to go. A less linear and more powerful way of thinking about vision is to view it as a surrounding field. Rather than a destination that pulls an organization forward, vision as a field permeates and guides the organization. As Margaret Wheatley (1992) says, "All employees . . . who bumped up against that field [of vision] would be influenced by it" (p. 54).

Developing a shared vision starts with clarifying your vision—and then mapping that to the organization's vision. What is your personal vision? How is it reflected in the organization's vision? The greater the alignment, the greater the force for achieving the vision.

Don't confuse vision and mission. Vision is knowing where you want to be or what you want to become. It includes tangibles, as seen in certain products in use throughout the country, as well as intangibles, such as virtues and the culture that you want to surround you. Vision is a collage of you and your organization in the future. Mission is your reason for being and the work you pursue to realize your vision. Your mission guides your actions to achieve what you envision for yourself and your organization. Both are necessary in life in general and especially for leaders of organizations.

▨ Reflection

Does your organization have both a vision and mission statement? How well do these statements drive decisions and actions? Are the vision and mission statements on a piece of paper tucked away in a drawer? Do they permeate your organization's culture and decision making on a daily basis? Do you have a vision for yourself and your family? Are you clear about your mission in life?

▨ Notes

_____

_____

_____

_____

_____

_____

_____

_____

_____

_____

_____

_____

_____

▨ DAY 5: Leading and Managing

Efficient management without effective leadership is "like straightening deck chairs on the Titanic."

—Stephen Covey

What is leadership and what is management?

Both are very important in organizational life and shouldn't be confused. Leadership is doing the right thing; management is doing things right. Managers direct the hacking of a new path through the jungle; leaders make sure that they are in the right jungle.

One of the major contributions that a leader can make is to always be able to distinguish between these two important functions. We often become so focused on the day-to-day realities of what we do that we lose sight of whether we are doing the right thing.

Leaders often have to ask the hard questions: Are we getting the best results possible? Do disparities in service or production need to be addressed? Are there ethical issues involved? What knowledge and skills does our staff need, and how will they get them? Will the proposed staff development give us what we need? Is our strategic planning council effective? These queries will help you challenge the status quo that is often accepted without question.

▨ Reflection

Think about the leadership role you play:

- Why are you doing what you are doing? What data do you have to show that you are solving the right problem?

- What aspects of your challenge require leadership? Needs management?

- Are you sure you are "doing the right things" before you set up procedures to "do things right"?

- What underlying assumptions seem to be driving your behavior? Are these consistent with where you want to be?

▨ Notes

▨ DAY 6: Processing Information

When asked what time it is do you say, it's about 9:00 or 8:52?

—Joyce S. Kaser

As a leader, how do you prefer to take in data? How do you know what you know?

Do you prefer to gather data by relying heavily on your five physical senses—what you can see, hear, taste, smell, and feel—in other words, that which you actually experience? Or do you prefer to rely on your hunches— the possibilities you imagine?

If your focus is on your immediate experience, you are tuned to the moment; you are realistic, practical, concrete, and detail oriented. You focus on the parts rather than the whole.

If your focus is on the meaning of your experience or what your experience could be, you are dealing with patterns and relationships. You are future oriented, imaginative, more abstract in your thinking, and focused on the big picture. You tend to see the whole rather than the parts.

These two preferences, sensing and intuition, describe the aspect of personality that deals with how we take in information, according to Carl Jung (1921/1971) and Isabel Briggs Myers (Myers et al., 1998).

If you have more of a sensing preference, you may tune into details and have great recall for facts, numbers, and names; but you may miss the connections among the data. If you are more intuitive, you may see the connections among information but may jump to conclusions that are not supported by data.

To be most effective as a leader, you need to be aware of your own strengths and compensate for your nonpreference. You can do this by knowing your preference and also being able to use your nonpreference as necessary. Your preference will always be where you start, but your nonpreference may be where you end up. You can also work with others so that both sensing and intuitive preferences are represented.

Your knowledge of the sensing/intuition polarity can be invaluable if you are using data to identify improvement efforts and make decisions about new programs and staff development.

▨ Reflection

What is your preference for gathering and making sense of information? How does it help or hinder you in your leadership role? What do you need to pay more attention to?

▨ Notes

▧ DAY 7: Managing Information

*An individual without information cannot take responsibility;
an individual who is given information cannot help but take
responsibility.*

—Jan Carlzon

What is one piece of quality information that changed your life?

Can you think of a circumstance in which you read a book, participated in a professional development experience, had a heart-to-heart talk with your supervisor, or discussed a problem with a colleague—and you came away with a completely new perspective that led you to take an action you wouldn't have taken otherwise?

Here are a few examples:

- "I really thought that my coworker Ed wasn't either very friendly or bright until I learned that he had a hearing problem. Once I knew that, my opinion of him—and how I conducted myself in his presence— changed completely."

- "Remember how people behaved when they thought the world was flat? They were afraid to go too far for fear of falling off the edge. Can you imagine what they thought when they heard for the first time that the world was round? What about the courage of the explorers who disproved this false information?"

- "Somehow, I made the link between the warning on TV and my symptoms. I'm here today because I got to the doctor early. Had I not done so, I'd likely be dead."

- "It was a rumor that turned out to be true. We heard that our company was about to be swallowed up by a large conglomerate. Not wanting that to happen, our president and board of directors made some strategic moves to prevent the takeover. We all still have our jobs because management acted quickly on this information."

The value of information is that it can change the way we think about something and therefore the way we act. It can lead us to change a habit, teach differently, sell one house and buy another, enroll in a master's program, decide to be a mentor, or make myriad other decisions.

▧ Reflection

It is critical for organizations undergoing change to have a free exchange of information. Here are some questions to ask yourself about the information available in your setting:

- Does your organization value the exchange of information? How do you know?

- Does each staff member have the information necessary to do his or her job?

- How does your organization handle bad news? Who gets the news? How is it shared?

- Is the information within your organization credible, accurate, and timely? How do you know?

- Does each staff member have the opportunity to provide feedback and to ask questions?

- Is information disseminated through a variety of channels (e.g., news-letters, presentations, electronically, face-to-face, etc.)?

- What organizational structures or mechanisms exist to generate and share new knowledge?

- What do you do personally to increase the exchange of information?

▨ Notes

_____

_____

_____

_____

_____

_____

_____

▨ DAY 8: Focusing on Customers

Consumers know more about what they want—and are more
determined to get what they want—than . . . ever . . . before.
—Jim Taylor

Think about a time you felt that you didn't get the service you wanted, needed, and deserved. Perhaps you had taken time off to have someone come fix an appliance and that person didn't show up and didn't call. Maybe you had paid a bill, but the accounting department kept sending you statements. Possibly you had made arrangements with your supervisor to take a personal leave day, but he or she had forgotten and scheduled you into a meeting.

Try to remember what you were feeling. Frustration? Anger? Resentment? Now, think of just the opposite situation.

Think about a time you were treated as a valued customer. Perhaps the accounting department notified you of an overpayment. Maybe someone from your clinic called to tell you that the doctor was running late. Possibly your supervisor stopped by to make sure that you had everything you needed to get the proposal in on time.

More and more leaders are asking their organizations to adopt a customer focus or consumer orientation. The customer is the person who is served, whose needs are satisfied by the service rendered.

Take education as an example. The ultimate customers are the students and the community. In the old paradigm, if students did not have basic skills in reading and mathematics, it was their fault. After all, they had the opportunity to learn, didn't they? If that situation occurs now, schools are more inclined to look at their own systems to determine what else can be done to ensure that the students reach their fullest potential. Their core mission is to teach students to read and write, not just to "deliver" lessons.

Students, their parents, and the community are external customers, but there are also internal customers—the colleagues with whom you work. It is important to treat colleagues as customers just as it is students and their parents. Sometimes, organizations treat their customers well but are much less attuned to the needs of their own staff.

Having a customer focus doesn't mean that your customers, both external and internal, will always be satisfied. That is an unrealistic expectation on their part and yours. Occasionally, a customer may be dishonest and be out to exploit you as the provider of a product or service. But for the most part, those instances are the exception. Having a customer focus means providing good service and making sure that people receive value.

▨ Reflection

Here are a few key questions to ask yourself to gauge your customer focus for both internal and external customers:

- Who are your customers—both internal and external?
- How customer focused are you?
- What do your customers value? How do you know?
- Are you providing them with value?
- What improvements are needed?
- How do you continuously assess customer satisfaction?

▨ Notes

_____

_____

_____

_____

_____

_____

_____

_____

▧ DAY 9: Making Decisions

Is this a matter of the head or the heart?

—Janet Theusen

As a leader, you make many important decisions during the course of each day. How do you go about doing so?

Some people prefer to decide by following the logic of a situation, taking a rather impersonal, objective stance. Others make a decision on the basis of its impact on people and their own subjective values.

If your focus is on objective decision making, you are likely to be analytical, value reason and justice, and question almost everything. If you prefer subjective decision making, you are likely to be appreciative, value compassion and harmony, and tend to be accommodating.

These two different orientations describe the aspect of personality that relates to how people make decisions, according to Carl Jung (1921/1971) and Isabel Briggs Myers (Myers et al., 1998). They call the polarities *thinking* (objective decision making) and *feeling* (subjective decision making). Note that the meanings of these two common words are different from the meanings normally associated with them. The focus is on subjective and objective decision making. Thinking, in this case, does not mean cognition nor does feeling refer to emotions.

Leaders need to get in touch with their preferred modes for making decisions and close the gap that overreliance on one mode may create for them. They can also help others better understand the dynamics of decision making.

For example, thinkers tend to embrace spirited discourse as a way to analyze situations, hammer out the logic, look at cause-and-effect relationships, and make objective decisions. Feelers often interpret this type of discourse as conflict, which they dislike and tend to avoid. They value harmony and see any kind of conflict—or perceived conflict—as a threat. They often opt for inclusivity as a means of avoiding conflict.

As a result of these two different orientations, those who prefer thinking and those preferring feeling often experience themselves as at odds with each other. This problem can be dealt with effectively and efficiently if approached as follows:

- Thinkers remember that feelers can see their robust debate as negative and off-putting.

- Feelers remember that an issue put on the table and dealt with is more likely to move a relationship or an organization forward than an issue that is repressed.

Your understanding of your own decision-making preference is critical for effective leadership. Dealing with differences constructively—regardless of your preference for decision making—is central to any reform effort.

▨ Reflection

What is your attitude toward conflict in your life? If you welcome it, be aware of those who are fearful and uncomfortable. Think of ways you can present your ideas in a less threatening way. If you avoid conflict, try moving toward it rather than running away. Normally, your fears are reduced by moving toward that which you fear rather than trying to avoid it.

▨ Notes

▨ DAY 10: Coping With Change

Entering the era of perpetual unrest means confusion, mixed feelings, and ambiguity are here to stay.

—Daryl Conner

Have you ever said something like, "Oh, my life will slow down when _____ is over"? We often hope that our lives will be more manageable, slower paced, or less hectic when some major event ends. What happens is that when one event is over, another takes its place. And they keep coming so that we never experience the respite we wish for.

The reality is that the days of small, incremental changes, which we could not only incorporate but often prepare for, are gone. As Daryl Conner (1998) describes, "The world is inundated with disruptions: unforeseen dangers, unanticipated opportunities, unmet expectations, alarming new statistics, startling twists of fate, shocking innovations, unheralded improvements, unrealistic requirements, overwhelming demands, contradictory directives, staggering liabilities, astonishing results, sudden strokes of luck, and more" (p. vi).

What, then, does it take for us to cope with continuous ambiguity, continuous change, and continuous confusion? Here are three major strategies:

Accept ambiguity, change, and confusion as the norm rather than the exception. The degree to which you experience stress is directly related to your expectations. If you expect your life to move slowly in a harmonious fashion, you may be upset when a meeting is canceled at the last minute, your car breaks down, or you leave your briefcase at the bank. If you know that you are subject to myriad forces and that the only thing you have control over is how you choose to react, you are much better equipped to deal with inevitable ambiguity, change, and confusion. Anchoring yourself in your core values and beliefs will give you additional support in weathering change.

Be resilient. Your ability to deal with the unknown is much greater if you have a high level of resiliency. Your outlook and attitude are important, as well as how you handle the daily stressors. Do you know how to release anger? Relieve frustration? Handle criticism and failure without internalizing? Do you eat properly, exercise, and get enough sleep? Are you a nonsmoker? Do you avoid drugs? Do you have a support system to rely on? Do you get away from work on a regular basis? These are all ways to be a resilient person, one who is capable of maintaining his or her productivity and quality standards along with physical and emotional stability while assimilating change (Conner, 1993).

Act anyway. Unless you are content to be paralyzed by your fear or to attempt escape to a more peaceful place and time, you have no choice other than to move ahead. Move ahead despite the continuous ambiguity, continuous change, and continuous confusion. Move forward with your fear and anxiety in hand rather than attempting to repress or escape from your feelings. Do each day the best you can.

Another way of saying this is to "Put a lion in your heart. 'To fight a bull when you are not scared is nothing,' says a well-known bullfighter, 'and not to fight a bull when you are scared is nothing. But to fight a bull when you are scared—that is something'" (von Oech, 1992, p. 51). What gives you the courage to act on your ideas? Having a well-thought-out plan? Encouragement? Faith in the idea? Past success? What puts a lion in your heart?

▨ Reflection

On a scale of 1 (low) to 10 (high), how do you rate your ability to cope with ambiguity and to assimilate change? Which of the three strategies listed above do you rely on to cope with major changes? What can you do to strengthen your capacity to deal with a constant state of flux? Do you know what puts a lion in your heart?

▨ Notes

_____

_____

_____

_____

_____

_____

_____

▨ DAY 11: Judging and Perceiving

What is your list-making behavior? Do you use them or lose them?
—Otto Kroeger

How do you prefer to go about living your life?

Do you prefer to organize your life and live in an orderly fashion with a plan? Or do you prefer to go with the flow and live in a spontaneous and flexible fashion?

If you prefer organization, you do a lot of planning, work from lists, are decisive, like structure, and usually push for closure. The downside of this preference includes decision and action without careful consideration of alternatives and much action with little reflection. On the other hand, if you are more spontaneous, you are adaptable, tolerate ambiguity well, are curious, and push to maintain openness. The downside of this preference includes lack of closure and the possibility that no decision is final and nothing is ever done.

These two preferences, judging and perceiving, describe the aspect of personality that deals with how people go about their lives, according to Isabel Briggs Myers (Myers et al., 1998). It is the preference that is often most visible to others. (Note that *judging* as used here is not synonymous with *judgmental*, the adjective). Which one is your preference?

Your preference for judging or perceiving is especially critical for your professional life. This dichotomy is the source of greatest tension in the workplace.

Here are a couple of tips for working effectively with people who prefer judging and those who prefer perceiving (Kroeger & Theusen, 1988):

Help people who prefer judging to incorporate unexpected items into their agenda by using the "hit and run" technique. People who prefer judging prefer their lives to be structured and ordered; they don't like surprises. However, much of life is unexpected and unpredictable, and judgers do have their schedules interrupted. The most effective way to "surprise" people who prefer judging is to drop something on them and then leave the area. (Using e-mail works well.) Give them time to incorporate the new item into their list, and they'll be fine. If you hang around while they do it, you deserve the flak you are likely to get.

Help people who prefer perceiving come to closure by determining the un-acceptable options. If you ask perceiving people their opinion or what they want, they may not know. The reason? They delight in generating options (and the more, the better) and oftentimes, have no need to make a choice unless forced to do so. If a choice is necessary, help them come to closure by ruling out unacceptable options. Deciding what they don't believe or don't want is easier than sorting out myriad attractive options.

Both of these tips work whether the two people involved have the same or different preferences in the judging/perceiving dichotomy.

▨ Reflection

Sometime today, try the tip for working with either judgers or perceivers. Make a note of what happened. As a leader, how can you use these tips to increase your effectiveness?

▨ Notes

_____

_____

_____

_____

_____

_____

_____

_____

▨ DAY 12: Networking

We cannot hope to influence any situation without respect for the complex network of people who contribute to our organizations.

—Margaret Wheatley

What networks are you part of, and what types of relationships do you have within these networks? How can you bring these relationships to bear on issues you care about?

There is a natural human desire to work in groups and to work well together. Information of all kinds is both generated and shared through networks of all types: organizational, professional, community, religious, and family. "Working the networks" is one way that leaders exert influence, communicate vision, share information, provide support, support continuity, and bring about change. Change in organizations is so complex that it cannot occur without strong relationships among people making up a variety of networks, some that exist within the boundaries of an organization and some that go outside.

A colleague who is a very successful businesswoman illustrates well the value of relationships within networks. She lives in a remote part of the country, does no marketing, has no letterhead stationery or brochures, and rarely uses a business card. Yet she has a thriving business. Her secret (which she says is no secret at all)? She does good work for her clients, and she maintains relationships. She gains, generates, and provides information through her networks; and her clients know that they can count on her to provide a high quality of service. As a result, she has a high level of repeat and referral business, which means that she doesn't have to market herself.

▨ Reflection

Which relationships provide you with diverse information and help you in your role as a leader of reform? Do you have relationships from different worlds that keep your mind open to new ideas and approaches and keep you from becoming too insular? What new relationships do you need to forge, and what networks do you need to become part of to broaden your influence?

▨ Notes

_____

_____

_____

▨ DAY 13: Leading With Principles

Example is leadership.

—Albert Schweitzer

What does it mean to model principle-centered leadership?

According to Stephen Covey (1992), principle-centered leaders operate in alignment with "self-evident, self-validating natural laws" (p. 19). These include such basic principles as fairness, equity, justice, honesty, trust, integrity, and service. These principles point the way for leaders. Covey refers to them as the compasses of organizations, in that they always point the way.

When people model principle-centered leadership, they follow these basic principles. Covey (1996) sees modeling as "a combination of character (who you are as a person) and competence (what you can do)" (pp. 151-152).

Leadership consists of three basic functions: pathfinding, aligning, and empowering (Covey, 1996, pp. 152-153):

1. Pathfinding links vision and mission with your value system and the needs of customers.

2. Aligning is making sure that organizational policies, practices, and systems contribute to the mission and vision of meeting the needs of customers and stakeholders.

3. Empowering is helping others discover and develop their talents.

▨ Reflection

Ask yourself these questions:

- What are your basic principles, and how do they shape who you are and what you do?

- What are the components of your own pathfinding?

- What components have you aligned? How do you know that they are aligned?

- How are you empowering others?

▨ Notes

_____

_____

_____

▨ DAY 14: Leadership Styles

Any type can be a leader, but not all types are proportionally represented among leaders.

—Otto Kroeger

What is your leadership style?

Are you best at visioning? Empowering others to act? Helping others develop their mission statements? Managing systems and procedures that allow others to do their work? Troubleshooting?

One way of looking at leadership styles is by using the typology based on the work of Carl Jung (1921/1971) and Isabel Briggs Myers (Myers et al., 1998). Which of the 16 different types are you? Do you prefer extraversion or introversion, sensing or intuition, thinking or feeling, or judging or perceiving? (If you are not sure, go back to Days 3, 6, 9, and 11.)

Of the 16 different types, 4 are overrepresented in leadership positions in organizations. They are ISTJ (Introversion-Sensing-Thinking-Judging), INTJ (Introversion-Intuition-Thinking-Judging), ESTJ (Extraversion-Sensing-Thinking-Judging), and ENTJ (Extraversion-Intuition-Thinking-Judging). People preferring these 4 types make up more than 62 percent of the leaders and managers in organizations of all kinds (Kroeger Associates, 2000): business, education, industry, the military, nonprofit, and service organizations. They are referred to as the "tough-minded executives" because of their shared preference for TJ (Thinking-Judging).

It may be that TJ behavior has become the norm for leaders. As a result, those having TJ preferences are more likely to be seen as leaders. However, the other 12 types can and do lead. In fact, as our society moves from transactional to transformative leadership (see Day 25), types such as the ENFP and ENFJ may have distinct advantages.

▨ Reflection

Think for a moment about your typological preferences:

- What are the strengths of your type as a leader in the workplace?
- What are the possible weaknesses of your type in the workplace?
- With whom can you work to complement your preferences and shore up any weaknesses?

▨ Notes

▨ DAY 15: Reframing Your Perspective

Too often [leaders and managers] bring too few ideas to the challenges that they face. They live in psychic prisons because they cannot look at old problems in a new light and attack old challenges with different and more powerful tools— they cannot reframe.

                              —Lee G. Bolman and Terrence E. Deal

One of the greatest skills a leader can bring to a group is the ability to reframe—simply because it is such a difficult task. We get so emotionally caught up in our own issues that we may not stop to think that reframing is possible. Actually, reframing may give us solutions we have never even thought of.

For example, how hard is it for you to replace "old data" with "new data"?

Think of a time when you wanted to think or feel differently about a person or situation. Even though you tried very hard, altering your frame of reference was very difficult, perhaps impossible.

There is good reason for that. Our frame of reference has two components: our expectations and our perceptions, which are integrally connected. As Daryl Conner (1998) points out, "We expect to get more of what we already see, and we usually can only see that which we already expect. That is why it is so difficult to move away from a perspective once it's established" (p. 317).

Through the act of reframing—deliberately looking at something through an entirely different lens—we can change our perceptions or our expectations. Any change in one will automatically produce a change in the other.

In changing our perceptions, we change the way we look at a situation. For example, you can look at a poor attempt at reform as a failure and look for someone to blame. Or you can look at what worked and what didn't and see the experience as a rich learning opportunity for the future.

If we can't change how we view the situation, we can always change our expectations. For example, if you expect the support of your supervisor in your reform effort and that support is not forthcoming, you will continue to experience frustration. An alternative is to accept the fact that support is not forthcoming and change your strategy.

Thus, in reframing, you purposefully look at the issue from a different angle or develop expectations that are more apt to resolve a situation.

▨ Reflection

Here are some ways to begin reframing:

- Get in touch with the lens (theory or assumptions) that underlies how you see the situation.

- Determine whether the lens is the right one for the situation. Which lens provides the greater opportunity for taking positive action?

- Expand your repertoire of lenses. Ask yourself how someone else would see this—a scientist? A child? A public official? A parent? A CEO of a major corporation?

Try reframing some issue that you are currently dealing with. Be conscious of whether you are altering your perceptions or expectations or both. What is the result?

▨ Notes

▨ DAY 16: Resolving Paradox

The contradictions of life are not accidental. Nor do they result from inept living. They are inherent in human nature and in the circumstances which surround lives.

—Palmer Parker

Inevitably, anyone in a leadership role encounters people and circumstances that reflect inherent contradictions. These are called *paradoxes.* Paradoxes stem from conflicting polarities: the existence of two opposing attributes, tendencies, or principles that are interdependent. For example, in large organizations, there is often tension between the desire to centralize and the desire to decentralize procedures and services. Having both operational in a system is the paradox. Another example is the need to work in teams versus working individually. Polarities and the paradoxes they create are ever present; they never go away.

Successful leaders know how to work through polarity disputes rather than trip over them. The first step in resolving a polarity conflict is knowing one's own biases. We tend to prefer one side of the polarity over the other. However, polarities are not "either/or;" they are "both/and" dilemmas. We must come to see the truth of both sides, recognizing the simultaneous existence of opposites.

If your organization is focusing on one side of a polarity as the solution to a problem, your role as a leader is to alert people to the other. For example, if your colleagues are pushing for a team structure, make sure to engage them in thinking about a more traditional structure. If they are advocating change, you can stress stability. If they are stressing diversity, you can emphasize unity. Your role as a leader is to balance both sides of the polarity and not allow one side to dominate to the exclusion of the other (Terry, in press).

▨ Reflection

What polarity conflicts do you see in your work? Which side of the polarity are you biased toward? What can you do to make sure that the other side of the polarity is considered and included?

▨ Notes

_____

_____

_____

▨ DAY 17: Working Synergistically

It takes an enormous amount of internal security to begin with the spirit of adventure, discovery, and creativity. Without doubt, you have to leave the comfort zone of base camp and confront an entirely new and unknown wilderness.

—Stephen Covey

What is synergy? Where does it come from? What value does it offer?

Synergy exists when the sum of something exceeds the whole of its parts. In an organizational context, it is an increase in effectiveness or achievement through cooperation or combined action of some type. People come together who have complementary skills and resources, and in combination, they can achieve far more than they could alone.

You can oftentimes experience synergy in a group. For example, a group will be exploring a solution to a problem. Some group members start the discussion. Others add their thoughts. All of a sudden, the group begins to see a path emerging. And as the way unveils itself, the excitement is almost palpable. The group continues to explore and adjust until the solution is clear, one that definitely would not have come into existence without the interaction of the group. It is unlikely that one person could have singularly devised the solution. Synergy "catalyzes, unifies, and unleashes the greatest powers within people" (Covey, 1989, p. 262).

What value does synergy offer to an organization? Working synergistically is most likely to produce results that are effective and satisfying, oftentimes highly creative. Working synergistically is more likely to produce win/win rather than win/lose solutions to problems because people negotiate what they will contribute and work toward until all are invested in a common goal. Working synergistically, then, requires greater involvement, which empowers people and increases their commitment to outcomes. Leaders working to improve teaching and learning need synergy among the many parts of the education system.

▨ Reflection

Think about a problem that you are now facing, especially a difficult one for which you can envision only a win/lose solution. How can you set up an exchange that might produce a different outcome? Who are the best people to participate in this discussion? What people share a stake in solving this problem? What conditions are needed to pull these people together and have a productive discussion?

▨ Notes

_____

_____

_____

_____

_____

_____

_____

_____

_____

_____

_____

_____

▨ DAY 18: Balancing the Whole

The opposite of a profound truth is also true.

—Richard Farson

One of the tensions in large organizations exists between the polarities of decentralization and centralization. Which decisions are made by the people at the top of the organization, and which ones are made by the people at different levels or locations?

Peter Senge and others advocate an organizational value called *localness* (Senge, Roberts, Ross, Smith, & Kleiner, 1994). According to this value, "A higher level should not make decisions for a lower level, if the lower level is capable of making the decision itself" (p. 309). This value builds responsibility from the bottom to the top of the organization. Decisions are made by those with the expertise who are closest to the situation.

Traditionally, those at the top of organizations set the policies and procedures, and those at lower levels carry them out. Localness unleashes "people's commitment by giving them the freedom to act, to try out their own ideas and be responsible for producing results" (Senge, 1990, pp. 287-288). The people at the lower levels are often much more knowledgeable about day-to-day operations and are in the best place to make decisions.

For example, teachers have traditionally been told by their supervisors which new programs to implement. After a while, the teachers may say the program isn't working, so those at the top chose a new program, and the cycle begins anew. In schools that value localness, teachers have the responsibility and power to ask what would work better and to help solve the problem. Leaders need to look for opportunities to challenge and empower people at all levels to solve the problems closest to them.

There are challenges for people at both the top and lower levels. No large organization can be controlled from the top. There are simply too many moving parts. People at the top need to recognize that their control is largely an illusion and be willing to give it up. Giving up control does not mean abandoning any role. Their new role is to build common vision and to support and facilitate this shared direction.

The value of localness must be balanced with the good of the whole. Senge (1990) discusses a phenomenon referred to as "The Tragedy of the Commons." This occurs when local decision makers, drawing on shared resources, focus only on their needs to the exclusion of the whole; they look at the closest part rather than the more distant whole. For example, a commercial orchard diverts water for irrigation, its immediate need, without considering how this decision affects other farmers farther down the river. In another example, a school selects a new curriculum without considering how it fits into the scope and sequence of the K-12 curriculum.

To guard against this phenomenon, someone who can influence local decision makers in the organization needs to be involved in making "commons" decisions. This is necessary because it is sometimes difficult for those at the local level to see the broader implications of their actions. Thus, centralization and decentralization can coexist in an accountable arrangement.

▨ Reflection

What decisions are best made at the level at which you are working? Which ones should be made at a lower level? At a higher level? Are you vulnerable to any "Tragedy of the Commons" misperceptions? How can you guard against these?

▨ Notes

_____

_____

_____

_____

_____

_____

_____

_____

▨ DAY 19: Sharing Vision

A shared vision is not an idea. . . . It is, rather,
a force in people's hearts, a force of impressive power.
—Peter Senge

As Day 4 points out, the concept of vision in organizations has almost become commonplace. Every organization has to have its vision and mission statements. Most visions, however, are not shared visions. They are imposed on others by the head of the organization or a group of people at the top. These visions are not effective long-term because they "command compliance—not commitment" (Senge, 1990, p. 206).

A shared vision is different. A shared vision incorporates individual visions, engenders commitment, and focuses energy. As Senge (1990) says, "When people truly share a vision, they are connected, bound together by a common aspiration. . . . Shared visions derive their power from a common caring" (p. 206).

Think about a time when you took part in developing a shared vision. Maybe it was for building a new house, raising a child, starting a new program in your organization, or turning around test scores in your district. What did having a shared vision feel like? Yes, you can actually feel shared visions; they are that powerful. People approach their work with greater enthusiasm and intense dedication.

How do shared visions come about? It is a process of cocreating. Here are some characteristics that describe this process:

- It is an ongoing process rather than a onetime event.
- Everyone involved in carrying out the vision participates in its generation.
- It involves a synthesis of individuals' personal visions.
- The process itself strengthens the leadership skills for those throughout the organization.
- The end result is a vision that has staying power and drives behavior over time.

Shared visions enable people to be bound by a common aspiration. There is reason to believe that shared visions evolve in part because of a strong underlying need for people to be connected in achieving some common goal. In fact, Senge (1990) says, "Few, if any, forces in human affairs are as powerful as shared vision" (p. 206).

▨ Reflection

List the shared visions—both personal and professional—that are part of your life. How does each provide purpose to your life and direct your behavior? If the reform effort you are leading has no shared vision, what can you do to engage people in building one?

▨ Notes

_____

_____

_____

_____

_____

_____

_____

_____

▨ DAY 20: Exploring Relationships

Relationships are all there is.

—Margaret Wheatley

Think about a relationship problem you have with a colleague or a member of your family. Can you pinpoint the underlying cause?

Regardless of whether the problems exist in organizations or in families, what often lies at the core of relationship problems is lack of clarity about or differences in roles and/or goals.

Consider this example: Several years ago, the organization that we (the authors) were part of hired a senior-level woman for a leadership role. We presumed that someone at her level would have certain knowledge and skills that she would use to bring in new business. After some time on the job, she had failed to provide leadership to the staff in existing work or to develop new contracts and business relationships. When confronted, she said no one had told her that that was her job.

Obviously, the source of our discomfort was our implicit expectation that she would be self-motivated and take initiative. In this example, the lack of clarity about an expectation is readily apparent. It is not, however, always that transparent. Sometimes, the conflict will focus on the problem rather than the underlying cause. Dealing with the discrepancy in expectations is likely to yield better results.

As a leader, you can have great influence in an organization if you constantly clarify roles and goals as a way of minimizing relationship conflicts in your organization. Find out what people expect of you and from the initiative you are leading. Assess how well their expectations match yours. Your leadership ability—that is, your ability to influence others—is directly related to your skill in building and maintaining relationships.

▨ Reflection

On a scale of 1 (low) to 10 (high), how do you rate your capacity to establish relationships? What are your strengths? Your weaknesses?

Now, think about your capacity to maintain relationships. (Usually people are better at establishing relationships than they are at maintaining them.) Using the same scale, what rating do you give yourself? What are your strengths and weaknesses in maintaining relationships? To what extent does your skill in clarifying roles and/or expectations contribute to your capacity to maintain relationships? If this is a problem, how can you be more explicit about what you want and ask for others to do the same?

▨ Notes

▨ DAY 21: Unity and Diversity

If we are to achieve a richer culture, rich in contrasting values,
we must recognize the whole gamut of human potentialities and
so weave a less arbitrary social fabric, one in which each diverse
human gift will find a fitting place.

—Margaret Mead

Unity versus diversity is a polarity set that has created great tension in organizations. Think for a moment about how your organization experiences this paradox.

Both unity and diversity make a contribution. Consider the following scenario: You meet a new staff member at the fall orientation. You quickly discover that this person graduated from your alma mater, has relatives in your hometown, lives two blocks away from you, and has children the same age as yours. Such similarities often facilitate a quick and immediate bond. The two of you agree to have lunch soon to get better acquainted.

Here is a different take: You meet a new staff member who was born in Peru. This person speaks fluent Spanish, is single with no children, has traveled extensively around the world, is a technology expert, and keeps two exotic birds as pets. You don't speak Spanish, are married with several children, haven't traveled outside the United States, are technology anxious, and are philosophically opposed to keeping exotic animals or birds as pets. You think that you have little in common with this person. Are you more likely to set up a lunch or walk away and meet someone else? If you are like most other human beings, you will move on to someone else. However, think for a moment how much you might learn from this person.

Preferring not to be anxious, people tend to avoid situations that are diverse culturally, ethnically, religiously, or in other ways. It is much less challenging to be with others of one's own culture, ethnicity, socioeconomic group, or religion. However, meeting people with varied backgrounds can offer the greatest learning opportunities. Leaders have a responsibility to model the value of associating with a variety of people.

That is why we need both diversity and unity for healthy organizational functioning. The unity provides the support and stability that make us feel comfortable. The diversity provides the challenge and diverse opinions that cause us to rethink our attitudes and beliefs and acquire new perceptions.

When an organization accentuates one polarity while minimizing the other, staff members are likely to feel the tension and may respond inappropriately. One of a leader's responsibilities is to fully explore both sides of any polarity set and help others feel more comfortable with the paradox that stems from embracing the two poles.

It is possible to forge unity within diversity through formal team-building activities as well as informal groupings and assignments. Use of the Myers-

Briggs Type Indicator is an effective way for leaders to help individuals build unity within diversity through understanding their own personality preferences and those of others.

▨ Reflection

What is the relationship between unity and diversity within your organization? To answer this broad question, consider the following:

- Who does the hiring in your organization? Who gets hired?

- How are work groups of various kinds structured?

- When people are free to choose, with whom do they select to work? What is the turnover rate in your organization? Does it differ based on race, ethnicity, sex, or other similar factors?

- Which holidays are observed?

- What kind of people are promoted?

- What is the racial, ethnic, and gender composition of your senior management team?

Answers to these specific questions will help you answer the bigger question on the relationship between unity and diversity. Do you believe that your organization is not sufficiently attending to one side of this polarity? If so, what can you do to help convey the importance of both unity and diversity?

▨ Notes

▨ DAY 22: Planning

Plans will get you into things, but you got to work your way out.

—Will Rogers

Imagine for a moment that you are headed off on a trip through unfamiliar territory. You have a vision of where you want to end up, a set of directions, and a day-by-day plan. Which of these three components can you most easily do without?

If you select the day-to-day plan, you are in agreement with management guru Stephen Covey (1989), who suggests that a clear destination and a compass are more important than a detailed plan. For a successful journey, knowing your destination and having a compass are key. That is because the plan will never be detailed and accurate enough for the ground you travel over. Also, there are too many possible interruptions (rain, a sprained ankle, an encounter with a bear) that can change the pace of the journey. However, if you know where you are going and have some guidance in getting there, a washed-out bridge or other obstacle will not deter you.

The same is true for change efforts in organizations. Having a very clear idea about the outcome you envision and a set of principles or general directions about how to achieve your outcome is more important for a successful reform effort than the detailed implementation plan. Organizational terrain is as subject as mountain terrain to environmental influences.

▨ Reflection

As you think about your reform effort, consider the following questions:

- Do you have a clear vision? Do you know when you will have achieved your desired outcome? What is the distance between where you are now and where you would like to be?

- What basic principles guide your reform effort? How apparent are these principles? What evidence do you have that they actually guide action?

- If you have a plan, how frequently is it revised? Do you (or others) spend more time on the plan than on the vision or the general direction of your reform effort?

▦ Notes

_____

_____

_____

_____

_____

_____

_____

_____

_____

_____

_____

▨ DAY 23: Breaking Static Patterns

The only true insanity is doing the same thing over and over and expecting different results.

—Rita Mae Brown

Think of a time you felt stymied by your attempts to change a frustrating or irritating situation. Have you found yourself doing the same thing over and over? Or perhaps the same thing with only slight variations? It is very human to do so, but not very effective. How do you break out of that mind-set?

In such situations, we often think that the problem is with the other person, people, or organization. However, we cannot control the behavior of anyone but ourselves. With that as a given, here are two different approaches for breaking the cycle:

Reframe the situation. You can turn a perplexing problem into a marvelous opportunity for learning by reframing. It is possible to transform what appears to be a failure into a test case, which failed in some ways, succeeded in others, and yielded great learning. The entry for Day 15 outlines such a reframing process.

Change your behavior. There are always myriad things you can do. Treat the person differently. Be kinder or firmer. Give more help or less help. Talk more or talk less. Be more independent or ask for help. If you are not sure what behavior to change, ask for advice from a trusted colleague.

Either reframing the situation or changing your behavior increases your chance of seeing some behavior change on the part of the other person. It is likely to work better than continuing to do whatever you have been doing or trying to get someone else to change his or her behavior.

▨ Reflection

Think of a time you repeated the same behavior but expected different results. Were you eventually able to break out of the pattern? If so, what happened? How do you recognize when you are caught in a cycle? Which of the above techniques is most useful in helping you respond differently?

▨ Notes

_____

_____

_____

_____

_____

_____

_____

_____

_____

_____

_____

_____

_____

▨ DAY 24: Positioning

Win/win is not a personality technique.
It's a total paradigm of human interaction.

—Stephen Covey

What is your typical operational paradigm for human interaction? Do you,

- Push for a win/win result?

- Opt for an outcome in which you win and someone else loses?

- Decide on a solution in which you lose and the other person wins?

- Settle for a result in which both of you lose?

- Select a solution in which you get what you want while leaving others to their own devices?

- State that the solution must be one of win/win or refuse to deal?

At times, each of these paradigms may be appropriate. For example, for a tennis match, a win/lose outcome is a given. It is the nature of the activity. In a situation in which you want to accommodate someone else, you may select a lose/win outcome. Sometimes, a win solution is totally appropriate. The best choice depends on the situation, and your challenge is to know what paradigm to use in which situation.

However, according to Covey (1989), most situations "are part of an in terdependent reality, and win/win is really the only viable alternative" (p. 211). So, if win/win (what some are now calling gain/gain) is the most desirable paradigm for most circumstances, what does this require?

According to Covey (1989), integrating a paradigm of win/win requires three character traits: integrity, maturity, and an orientation of abundance mentality. Integrity is the value placed on self—knowing one's values and making and keeping commitments. Maturity is "the balance between courage and consideration" for others (p. 217). Abundance mentality is an orientation to the notion that there is more than enough to go around. Lacking an abundance mentality results in seeing everything as a "zero sum" game. To engage in synergistic partnership requires that both parties value sharing their resources toward the greater good.

Covey (1989) also says that an open relationship needs to exist for a win/win option to occur, as well as performance agreements that shift people from a hierarchical to a "partners in success" status (pp. 216-223).

Operating out of a win/win paradigm seems easy, maybe even simplistic. In reality, it is actually very complex. Most people tend to think in "either/or" terms, and "both/and" thinking is more difficult. Ask yourself what you have to gain from a situation. What do others have to gain? What does anyone have to lose? Is there a way to minimize the loss and maximize the gain?

▨ Reflection

Think of your most recent situation. Did you operate from a win/win position or some other? If so, which one? If you didn't operate from a win/win orientation, would it have been appropriate? If so, how might the outcome have been different? What do you need to do to more fully integrate a win/win paradigm?

▨ Notes

_____

_____

_____

_____

_____

_____

_____

_____

_____

▩ DAY 25: Transactional and Transformational Leadership

Just like everything else in our society today, our understanding of leadership is changing. As conditions in our world have changed, our knowledge of the characteristics of effective leaders has evolved.

—James MacGregor Burns

Traditionally, leadership has been transactional, and it still is. Leaders inform followers as to what is expected from them and what they will receive for performing appropriately. In a reform effort, the leaders set the visions and clarify the roles of followers in achieving the vision. The leader also makes explicit the rewards followers will receive if they work to achieve the vision. Convinced of either the worthiness of the effort or the value of the rewards they will receive (or both), the followers then carry out their roles.

Emerging recently as a very different approach, transformational leadership is more complex and powerful. (In fact, transactional leadership and transformational leadership are often seen as two ends of a continuum.) In this approach, transformational leaders seek out the views of their followers and involve them on a more regular and personal basis. This is the type of leadership present when an organization develops a shared vision (see Day 19).

This approach to leadership is based on Maslow's hierarchy of needs (1954). According to this hierarchy, once one level of needs has been fulfilled, a person wants to fulfill needs on the next level. The highest needs include developing one's talents, interests, skills, and abilities. People cannot address these needs, however, until their basic physiological and psychological needs have been met. Once basic needs are satisfied, people are freer to develop their capability and potential. In other words, they move up Maslow's hierarchy from a survival to a fulfillment level.

Morals and ethics belong to another dimension of leadership that is more prevalent in the workplace. For example, adding this aspect helps answer the question of whether Adolf Hitler was a leader. Two key aspects of leadership are (a) having clear moral and ethical standards and (b) taking responsibility for one's decisions and actions (Bybee, 1993).

▩ Reflection

Which approach to leadership are you most familiar with? Which do you feel is most aligned with your own values? If you want to change something about your approach to leadership, what would it be? What can you do if your approach is more transformative and that of others in your organization is more transactional?

▨ Notes

▨ DAY 26: Examining Your Beliefs

> *The insidious effect of taken-for-granted assumptions is the way they interconnect with and reify one another in a seemingly logical set of relationships . . . If, on the other hand, educators begin with a belief in the transformative role of education, the value of accessing diversity, a faith in the potential success of every student, a commitment to collaborative and political linkages with parents and communities, then mustering the inventiveness to create new ways of organizing on behalf of children would be the logical, moral, and just thing to do.*
>
> —From *An Essay Review of Challenges to Dominant Assumptions controlling Educational Reform*, Terry A. Astuto et al.

In reflecting back on her early days, a former teacher told the following story:

> It was a day I'll never forget and an important lesson learned. I was a first-year teacher, only slightly older than my students. In the study hall I was in charge of, there was a young man who would not stop disrupting others through his talking. I recalled another teacher relating a very successful incident he'd had in taping students' mouths shut when they wouldn't be quiet. In my increasing frustration, I grabbed a roll of tape and approached this young man. All of a sudden, I realized that he was bigger than I was, and that did make a difference. Also, I saw this technique as incongruous with what I believed about how to treat students. In my moment of need, I lost my own grounding and grabbed someone else's approach.

How many times do we do something because someone else has done it, because we have always done it this way, or because some important person suggested it? We often act without considering whether our behavior is congruent with our underlying assumptions, or we don't question our assumptions. These behaviors are often deterrents to reform. The anecdote shows how acting without checking one's underlying assumptions can result in bad choices.

Here is a chance for you to determine your basic assumptions about leadership: Do you believe that (a) leaders are born or (b) leaders are made? That (a) leadership is positional (i.e., based on their positions, only certain people in organizations are leaders) or (b) everyone in an organization can exert leadership? That (a) leadership exists independently of ethics (e.g., Hitler was a leader) or (b) leadership is inherently ethical (e.g., Hitler was not a leader)?

Does your behavior indicate that you believe that certain people are blessed at birth with leadership abilities? Or do you act as if everyone can learn to exhibit some degree of leadership if they choose to? Do you see that leadership is vested in people with certain titles, or do you believe in the leadership capacity within all people in an organization? In your belief system, what is the relationship between leadership and ethics? You should be able to tie your behavior to one of the assumptions in each pair. Is your behavior congruent with what you believe, or have you fallen into a pattern of acting inconsistently with what you believe?

▨ Reflection

Think for a moment about how you are leading your reform effort. What assumptions do your behaviors support? Are they the assumptions that you truly hold?

▨ Notes

_____

_____

_____

_____

_____

_____

_____

▨ DAY 27: Communicating

Leaders communicate more than other people in a group.

—Max DePree

Leading is hard work. Those deemed leaders (either through their position or their influence) communicate all the time. Sometimes, this communication is conscious and intentional. More often, however, it is unconscious and unintentional. Each day, leaders perform thousands of symbolic acts that, regardless of their size, ripple through organizations and have profound effects. The behavior of leaders is always being observed and interpreted.

Here are some of the different ways leaders communicate:

- Body language (gestures, posture, touching, standing, facial expressions)

- Physical presence, including dress

- Ability and willingness to listen

- Accessibility and openness

- Words (written and spoken)

- Behavior (has a vision, walks the talk, uses good judgment, communicates with the right persons)

Organizations need leaders who send clear, coherent, consistent, and appropriate messages. If leaders are vague, inconsistent, or noncommittal, followers are likely to be confused and lose connection with the leader and the organization's vision and mission.

By paying undue attention to the medium through which they communicate, leaders run the risk of focusing on style more than on substance. In reality, "There is no perceived substance without symbols" (Peters, 1987, p. 420). People build trust and credibility through observing leaders' behavior—not by reading their policy documents.

▨ Reflection

Think of the ways you communicate. Assess yourself against the list above. Are you readily accessible? Do you have a strong physical presence? Do you have a vision? Are you a good listener? Is there congruity between your words and actions? How can you strengthen your communication skills as a leader?

▨ Notes

_____

_____

_____

_____

_____

_____

_____

_____

_____

_____

_____

_____

▨ DAY 28: Knowing Your Organizational Culture

Any organization that sets out to change its own culture
remains powerfully influenced by that culture
even as it attempts the change.

—Robert Evans

What is the culture of your organization?

Daryl Conner (1993) defines *culture* as "the beliefs, behaviors, and assumptions of an organization [that] serve as a guide to what are considered appropriate or inappropriate actions" for individuals and groups to engage in (p. 164). Culture operates at two levels: (a) overtly, as apparent in policies and procedures and (b) covertly, reflected in "the way things are done."

Culture in an organization usually evolves over time. The personalities of the leaders often determine the beliefs, behaviors, and assumptions that eventually become firmly established, although they may not be especially visible. This results in what Conner (1993) calls a "default" culture.

It is much less common for leaders to consciously and deliberately establish the type of organizational culture that serves their needs. As a result, new leaders often inherit a culture that doesn't support changes they want to make in the organization. And they find out quickly that a nonsupportive culture can quickly kill a change initiative.

If you are a leader of a new organization or project, you have the opportunity to build the type of culture you believe works best. If you take over an existing entity, you have the harder task of assessing and changing the culture—a difficult but not impossible task.

Regardless of which position you are in, what is it that you are attempting to mold? Here is a list of questions about organizational culture:

- What guides organizational decisions and behaviors? Is it a set of values and principles or the personality of the leaders?

- What is the trust level in the organization? Do people at different levels trust one another?

- Are people valued as individuals or are they thought of primarily as assets or resources?

- Are people's hands, heads, and hearts wanted—or just their hands?

- Does the organization promote egalitarianism, or does it rely on status, with a belief in superiors and inferiors?

- Is the atmosphere informal and comfortable, or is it formal and tense?

- Are people treated equitably, or is there evidence of preferential treatment?

- Is the environment positive, with people encouraged and recognized? Is it negative, with little or no recognition and a lot of blaming?

- Are employees treated as well as customers, or do leaders and managers receive special treatment?

- Does the organization freely share information, or is the information flow tightly controlled?

- Is learning from mistakes valued, or are people more likely to be fired or reprimanded for errors or failure?

- Is learning valued, or is it seen as a deterrent to getting the work done?

- Is the organization committed to continuous improvement, or does it change only when there is a major problem?

- What parts of the organizational culture should be preserved?[1]

▨ Reflection

Can you identify the culture of your organization? Is it firmly set or still relatively malleable? Does it support or hinder your reform efforts? Are you in a position to help establish or change the culture? If so, what would be your top three priorities?

▨ Notes

_____

_____

_____

_____

_____

_____

▧ DAY 29: Problem Solving

By paying attention to all four [functions],
a better decision results.

—Sandra Krebs Hirsh and Jean M. Kummerow

Think back to a recent problem you were trying to solve. Do you recall how you went about it?

There are four important factors to look at in problem solving. Leaving out one or more will usually produce a decision that won't stand the test of time. Here is what should be included:

- *Examine the facts.* What do you know about the problem? What is current and real?

- *Consider the possibilities.* Consider possible causes of the problem, alternative solutions, or both. Use the most imaginative thinking available.

- *Evaluate the situation logically.* Perhaps this involves making a list of the pros and cons of any possible solution or analyzing cause-and-effect relationships (i.e., if you do *x*, then *y* is likely to happen).

- *Look at the impact of your proposed solution on people, including yourself and your own value set.* How will your solution affect other people? Yourself? Is it congruent with your value system? Is this what you really want for yourself and your organization?

These four factors correspond to the four functions of personality (sensing/intuition/thinking/feeling) as set forth by Carl Jung (1921/1971) and Isabel Briggs Myers et al. (1998). (See Days 6 and 9.)

Here is an example of the importance of these factors in making decisions: A director of a professional association fired a relatively new employee who had falsified 15 minutes on her time sheet. He took this one fact, that she had misrepresented 15 minutes, and used it as the basis for letting her go. At no time did he consider any extenuating circumstances that might have led to her falsifying her time. Neither did he consider the impact of his decision on his staff, who marched into his office demanding to know why he had taken such brash action. This young woman had performed well and had much support within the organization.

As the story unfolded, the director discovered that the woman had not known how to record her brief absence and had done so incorrectly. There was no malicious intent on her part. The director called her to apologize and to ask her to return. It was too late; she was angry at the way she had been treated and had found another job. In this case, he had relied on looking at a fact and evaluating it logically, ignoring possibilities and the impact on people. Had he considered these two other factors, he would likely have made a different decision.

▩ Reflection

Just like the man in the story, most of us rely on two of these four factors in making decisions, often to the exclusion of the other two. Which two are your favorites? They are likely to correspond to the personality preferences you identified for yourself in Days 6 and 9. Which two are you most likely to ignore or skip over? Those probably represent the preferences you didn't identify for yourself.

Think of a problem you are facing. Work through a solution the way you normally do. Now, take into account all four functions, following the guidelines listed above. Is the resolution different? If so, how?

▩ Notes

_____

_____

_____

_____

_____

_____

_____

_____

▨ DAY 30: Choosing a Power Base

Leaders are leaders only as long as they have the respect and loyalty of their followers.

—Hans Selye

What do you think of when you hear the word *power* being used in relation to people, as in "She's a powerful woman" or "He's got a lot of power in this organization"?

Power is simply the ability or capacity to make and keep decisions over time. In and of itself, it is neutral. It can be used appropriately and inappropriately. Our feelings about power are tied into our experiences, and some of those may not be positive.

Stephen Covey (1992) looks at power from the perspective of followers rather than leaders and sees three different types. When a leader uses coercive power, followers follow because they are afraid. They will either be punished in some way or lose something if they fail to do what the leader wants. When a leader relies on utility power, followers follow because of the benefits they will receive if they comply. Based on the exchange of goods and services, this type of power is the most common. If leaders use legitimate power, followers follow because they believe in the leaders, trust them, and want to achieve the same ends. This type of power is used much less often.

Each type of power has different consequences. Coercive power relies on fear and will work only as long as there is something to be feared. Although it is based on equity, utility power generates a reactive response from followers, albeit usually a positive reactive response. It often encourages individualism rather than group efforts. Legitimate power relies on mutual respect and honor and produces a sustained, proactive response from followers.

The essential choice leaders must make is deciding which power base to operate from. The choice will reflect the leader's character as well as his or her past experiences and level of relationship skills.

▨ Reflection

Pay attention to your own language. Do you often cite the consequences of noncompliance, as in "Those who fail to do this will . . ."? If so, you may be drawing on coercive power. Do you make promises, as in "Those who do this will get extra credit, a raise, a bonus . . ."? If so, you may be relying on utility power. Pay attention to the times you may use these words and think about whether it would be more effective to build trust and commitment so people are more motivated to make desired changes.

After considering the above questions, what type of power base do you see yourself relying on most frequently? How do followers respond? What

type of power base would you prefer to use more often? How do you think
followers would respond?

▨ Notes

_____

_____

_____

_____

_____

_____

_____

_____

_____

_____

_____

▧ DAY 31: Doing the Right Thing

Neither let us be slandered from our duty by false accusations against us, nor frightened from it by menaces of destruction to the government, nor of dungeons to ourselves. Let us have faith that right makes might, and in that faith let us to the end dare to do our duty as we understand it.

— Abraham Lincoln

How do you know you are doing the right thing?

This is a question that leaders often face. Anyone taking on a leadership role will be subject to criticism, some of it unjust. In fact, if you are not experiencing some measure of criticism, chances are that you are not exerting much leadership. By being critical, others express and to some extent relieve their anxiety about the potential impact of your leadership efforts on them. Their criticism usually says more about where they are than where you are.

However, unless we have developed very thick skins, most of us feel the sting of the criticism. The best response is to acknowledge and reflect on the criticism and then press on. At the same time, it is very normal for us to ask ourselves whether we are doing the right thing. Although this is a question that ultimately only you can answer, there are questions you can ask yourself to make sure you have made the right decision.

▧ Reflection

If you need to do some soul-searching about your efforts to bring about reform, here are some questions to ask yourself:

- Is your vision grounded in research and the experience of professionals whose work you know and respect? Is your reform effort congruent with best practice? Have you touched base with those who are more experienced?

- Is your effort based on solid ethical principles? Have you thoroughly examined all aspects of your reform effort for any ethical issues?

- Do you have sufficient support? Although throughout history individuals have accomplished remarkable feats alone, the likelihood of a single person transforming a large organization is slim. The existing system is set up in a way that makes that very difficult to happen. Therefore, you do need a support base.

- Are factors in place that will enable your leadership efforts to be successful? Is your vision clear? Do you have sufficient resources—both material and human? Is the timing right?

- *Are you doing it because it needs to be done?* How much of your own ego do you have invested in this? Chances are, there is an inverse relationship between how right the reform effort is and how much of your ego you have invested. And remember, investing yourself and investing your ego are very different.

Your answers to these questions should give you some guidance in knowing whether you are doing the right thing. However, there are no automatic guarantees; you have no idea what tomorrow will bring. All you can do today is to lead with authenticity and the compelling belief that what you are doing is right. Ultimately, by checking your progress along the way and keeping your eye on the horizon, you will know.

Notes

_____

_____

_____

_____

_____

_____

_____

_____

Note

1. This list of questions was adapted from an unpublished instrument, "Classical Bureaucracy and High Performance System Choices," developed by Bruce Gibb (n.d.).

Bibliography

Burns, J. M. (1978). *Leadership.* New York: Harper & Row.

Bybee, R. W. (1993). *Reforming science education.* New York: Teachers College Press.

Conner, D. R. (1993). *Managing at the speed of change.* New York: Villard Books.

Conner, D. R. (1998). *Leading at the edge of chaos.* New York: John Wiley.

Covey, S. R. (1989). *The 7 habits of highly effective people.* New York: Simon & Schuster.

Covey, S. R. (1992). *Principle-centered leadership.* London: Simon & Schuster.

Covey, S. R. (1996). Three roles of the leader in the new paradigm. In I. F. Hesselbein, M. Goldsmith, and R. Beckhard (Eds.), *The Leader of the future.* San Francisco: Jossey-Bass.

Dixon, N. M., & Ross, R. B. (1999). The organizational learning cycle: Turning knowledge creation into a self-changing system. In Senge, P. M., Kleiner, A., Roberts, C., Ross, R. B., Roth, G., & Smith, B. J., *The dance of change.* New York: Doubleday.

Jung, C. J. (1971). *Psychological types.* Princeton, NJ: Princeton University Press. (Original work published 1921)

Kroeger, O. & Theusen, J. M. (1988). *Type talk.* New York: Delacorte.

Kroeger, O. (with Theusen, J. M.). (1992). *Type talk at work.* New York: Delacorte.

Kroeger, O. (2000). *Myers-Briggs type indicator qualifying workshop binder.* Fairfax, VA: Otto Kroeger.

Maslow, A.H. (1954). *Motivation and personality.* New York: Harper.

Myers, I. B., McCaulley, M. H., Quenk, N. L., & Hammer, A. L. (1998). *MBTI manual.* Palo Alto, CA: Consulting Psychologists Press.

Peters, T. (1987). *Thriving on chaos: Handbook for a management revolution.* New York: Knopf.

Senge, P. M. (1990). *The fifth discipline.* New York: Doubleday.

Senge, P. M., Roberts, C., Ross, R. B., Smith, B. J., & Kleiner, A. (1994). *The fifth discipline fieldbook.* New York: Doubleday.

Terry, R. (in press). *The challenges of leadership.* San Francisco: Jossey Bass.

von Oech, R. (1992). *Creative whack pack.* Stamford, CT: U.S. Games Systems.

Wheatley, M.J. (1992). *Leadership and the new science.* San Francisco: Berrett-Koehler.

Book Two

Leading Change

This book is a collection of thoughts and inspirations on leading change efforts. Often, the principal role of the leader is to recognize that change is needed, design the best map for change, and move people down the road. These 31 contemplations contain information about current research and practice on managing change in organizations.

The contemplations explore a number of key questions about change. Where do changes in organizations originate? Why do people experience the same change differently? What factors in our society contribute to the increasing rate of change? In any major change effort, what aspects of an organization need to remain stable? What motivates people to change? What are the stages of change? What is the role of vision in a change initiative? Who should be involved in a major change effort?

And the questions continue. Why is resistance a natural phenomenon, and how can it be useful in guiding a change effort? Why is an organization's change history important in determining the success of a current change initiative? Is it possible to determine an organization's readiness for change? What is the leader's role in modeling behaviors that support change?

The questions are grouped around four major themes: (a) Change is a process that should and can be managed; (b) organizations change only when the people within them change; (c) leaders have a set of responsibilities in directing change; and (d) change is systemic, and the organization as well as its people need to be attended to in any change initiative.

PART I
Planning and Directing

Change is not a process that simply unfolds; it must be planned and guided. Two major ideas underlie the contemplations in this section. One is that change is a process. Successful change initiatives evolve over time from initiation to implementation and, finally, to institutionalization. Both organizations and individuals experience various stages in the change process.

The second idea is that change can and must be planned and guided or managed. Planning for the entire change initiative is critical. Following a cycle such as "Plan, Do, Check, and Act" (Senge et al., 1999) helps leaders attend to changing circumstances and make necessary adjustments along the way.

◧ DAY 1: Change as Process

Change is a process, not an event.
— Gene Hall and Shirley Hord

What is the difference between an event and a process? An event is a onetime occurrence. It happens; and it is over and done with. In contrast, a process is ongoing. It takes place over time and evolves. In fact, it often has predictable stages.

How do people treat change as a onetime event? The following are some typical illustrations:

- Send out a memo saying that from this point on, this is how things will be done
- Invest in a new program and expect that people will automatically be able to use it
- Send people off for training and expect them to immediately behave differently
- Enact a new policy or practice and then announce it to the staff
- Offer people professional development with the expectation that they will successfully help others
- Involve only a small number of people in making the change instead of a more broadly based group of stakeholders
- Expect to see immediate results for a change initiative

When people treat change as an event, it is doomed to fail. Unless the change is one of minimal consequence, it simply won't happen. What is different when people see change as a process? They do the following:

- Involve the people affected by the change in planning for the change
- Account for the impact of change on the people involved
- Know that any significant change takes time and plan accordingly
- Employ professional development over time to ensure that people acquire the right knowledge and skills to implement the change
- Set realistic expectations for implementation
- Apply a monitoring procedure to track key benchmark events

Viewing change as a process increases the likelihood of obtaining the desired results.

▨ Reflection

Recall one or more examples in your organization in which change was treated as an event. How did that occur? What was the end result? How did people feel about what happened?

Are there examples from your organization in which change was treated as a process? What was different?

As a leader, what actions can you take that model change as a process rather than as an event?

▨ Notes

_____

_____

_____

_____

_____

_____

_____

_____

_____

▨ DAY 2: Stages of Change

The interval between the decay of the old and the formation and
the establishment of the new, constitutes a period of transition
which must always necessarily be one of uncertainty, confusion,
error, and wild and fierce fanaticism.

—John C. Calhoun

Development through a sequence of stages applies to much of human behavior. We talk about developmental stages that children go through as they grow and mature. There are also documented stages experienced by adults as they mature and age.

When we consider change—either personal or organizational—the concept of stages also applies. Elisabeth Kübler-Ross's (1970) well-known work concerned the stages of grief experienced by individuals as they adjust to a loss. Beverly Anderson (1993, pp. 14-15) documented six stages through which people proceed during systemic change:

- *Maintenance of the old system.* People are unaware that their organizations no longer operate in a way that serves the needs of clients and stakeholders. They do not know of or fail to acknowledge that new information exists.

- *Awareness.* Some stakeholders become aware that the organization is not functioning as it should but aren't sure what to do about it.

- *Exploration.* A more broadly based group in the organization tests some new ways of managing and doing the work, usually in low-risk situations.

- *Transition.* A critical number of key individuals in the organization pledge themselves to the new system and take higher-level risks to institutionalize the new ways.

- *Emergence of a new infrastructure.* Some elements of the new approaches have been institutionalized. There is a broad-based acceptance of the new system.

- *Predominance of the new system.* The new system replaces the old system. Key individuals support the new system and now embrace continuous improvement.

A delineation of these stages helps us understand two basic facts about change.

Change takes time. An organization does not progress through these six stages in a week or a month. Months and years are often necessary to make a complete transition.

Change is not necessarily linear or even. Brownian motion is common. (*Brownian motion,* originally a scientific term, refers to the irregular movement of microscopic particles suspended in a fluid.) Going back and forth between stages or around and around are typical of both personal and organizational change. It is often three steps forward followed by two back, but ideally, overall progress toward change continues.

▧ Reflection

Think of a change initiative that was carried out in your organization. Can you chart its growth and development?

- What caused the change effort to move beyond Stage 1—maintenance of the status quo?
- Where is it now?
- Has it gone through certain stages? If so, which ones? What evidence do you have?
- How long has it taken your organization to move through these stages?
- Did it get stuck at any point? What forces moved the initiative along?
- Is it continuing to move forward?
- What can help it move faster?

Here is another set of important questions:

- What has been your role in helping your organization move through these stages?
- What can you do to facilitate further growth within your organization?

▧ Notes

_____

_____

_____

_____

▨ DAY 3: Individual Change

Change is made by individuals first, then institutions.

—Susan Loucks-Horsley

Just as organizations move through stages in a change initiative, so do individuals.

The Concerns-Based Adoption Model (CBAM; Hall & Hord, 2001) is one model that has delineated the stages of use that individuals typically go through in implementing an innovation. This model lists seven levels of use and common behaviors associated with each level (see Table 2.1).

Table 2.1 The Concerns-Based Adoption Model (CBAM): Levels of Use And Behavioral Indices

Levels of Use	Behavioral Indices of Level
VI: Renewal	The user is seeking more effective alternatives to the established use of the innovation.
V: Integration	The user is making deliberate efforts to coordinate with others in using the innovation.
IVB: Refinement	The user is making changes to increase outcomes.
IVA: Routine	The user is making few or no changes and has an established pattern of use.
III: Mechanical	The user is using the innovation in a poorly coordinated manner and is making user-oriented changes.
II: Preparation	The user is preparing to use the innovation.
I: Orientation	The user is seeking out information about the innovation.
O: Non-use	No action is being taken with respect to the innovation.

SOURCE: From Hall & Hord, *Implementing Change: Patterns, Principles, and Potholes.* Copyright © 2001 by Allyn & Bacon. Reprinted by permission.

Obviously, for any organization to change, the individuals who implement the change effort must change, and their leaders must support them in this process and often make the change themselves.

▨ Reflection

Go back to the organizational change effort that you recalled for the previous day's contemplation and answer the following questions:

- Have you experienced any of the stages listed above? If so, which ones?

- If you didn't experience the stages yourself, can you identify them in other people?
- If you were a leader, did you personally implement the change or merely support others in doing so?
- Given this knowledge of the stages through which individuals pass, what might you do differently in leading your next change initiative?

▨ Notes

_____

_____

_____

_____

_____

_____

_____

_____

_____

▨ DAY 4: Using Data to Guide Change Efforts

Providing people with data before asking for their opinions and ideas . . . leads to different responses and outcomes. Possession of such information frequently requires individuals to reexamine their assumptions.

—Shirley D. McCune

If you are a seasoned professional, think back to earlier days in your career. Did you collect data to inform your decisions? If so, what data did you collect? Did you use the data? If so, in what ways? If you collected and used multiple data sources in the past, you are the exception rather than the rule.

One of the basic concepts of change management is data-based decision making. It helps you to pinpoint problems and begin to consider alternative solutions. For example, if you know that the students who score below the 50th percentile in reading typically do not attend the district's preschool program, you may want to increase participation in the preschool program. However, because there are other variables that may be contributing to the students' lower performances, you can't conclude that the program alone is producing the result. You will want to explore other interventions, such as strengthening the reading program in the early grades and/or working with preschool parents on reading readiness strategies. Gathering additional data will help you to know which of these interventions are responsible for achieving the desired result.

In addition to knowing what actions to take, data reveal how your change initiative is progressing and what you need to do differently to stay on target. In the above example, monitoring the number and type of students actually enrolled in the preschool program tells you whether your recruiting efforts are effective.

One of the essential components of change management is setting up information systems for decision making. Data are collected and analyzed prior to and after decision making. This enables all stakeholders to have the same information base. Such a database needs to exist at the organizational level as well as at the unit or departmental level because different decisions are made at different levels.

▨ Reflection

As a leader, consider your uses for data:

- Do you model the use of data for decision making in any change initiative that your organization undertakes? If so, how? If not, why not?

- Do you base your decisions on data and then monitor to check the results of your actions?

- What data do you find particularly helpful? Do you collect data that you really don't need?

- Do you "cast a wide net" with data collection to ensure that you gather information about the issue from a variety of perspectives?

- What data would you like to have that isn't available right now?

- Are the data accurate? Timely? In a form that is user-friendly?

If your organization does not use data in initiating and tracking change efforts, what can you do to promote the application of data-based decision making?

▨ Notes

_____

_____

_____

_____

_____

_____

_____

_____

▨ DAY 5: Planning for Change

We think in generalities, but we live in detail.

—Alfred North Whitehead

How concrete are the details regarding your change initiative? Are these details set forth in a written plan?

Are the people involved in formulating the change initiative cognizant of
what is happening and when? Is there a timetable? Do people know what they
are supposed to do? Have benchmarks been set up to gauge progress? Are organizational supports in place for institutionalization? Are there criteria for
success?

And most important, is the plan flexible? Can it be adjusted in response to
unanticipated events? Is it reviewed and adjusted regularly? Are revisions to
the plan communicated to others involved in the change initiative?

A component in managing successful change is having a plan for each
stage. Such a plan details what steps will be taken, by whom, at what point,
and to what end. A plan has the following purposes or dimensions:

- Sets forth desired outcomes
- Serves as a guide for achieving those outcomes
- Provides a means for others to monitor how well a change effort is
  progressing
- Documents the degree of alignment that exists between the vision,
  mission(s), goals, and activities
- Serves as leverage for binding different parts of an organization
  together
- Sets forth evaluation criteria

A plan for any stage is not cast in stone. As change efforts evolve, the plan
is revised; that is the nature of organizational change. As the contemplation
for Day 22 in Book One points out, the overall direction and guiding principles are always more important than the details. However, as each next step
comes closer in time, the details become more important. Flexibility is the
key. A dynamic plan continually serves as a guide for all to follow.

▨ Reflection

Does your organization have a documented plan (or plans) for its change
initiative? Is it a working document that the staff uses and regularly updates?
Who is the custodian of the plan? Who knows about the plan and has access to
it? Do evaluation and reflection activities inform revisions to the plan?

If you answered any of these questions "No," what can you do to encourage your organization to develop a working plan?

▨ Notes

_____

_____

_____

_____

_____

_____

_____

_____

_____

_____

▨ DAY 6: Change as Continuous Improvement

May your children live in a time of change.

—Ancient Chinese curse

How is change viewed in your organization? Is it readily embraced, or has it become a dirty word?

There is the danger that change will take on a negative connotation if your organization isn't careful about how it approaches change. One reform effort after another, all of which have potential for significant impact, may cause your staff to dread the next announcement. They may be—or at least think they are—on their way to burnout. And that is especially true if change is approached as an event rather than a process.

One possible alternative is to frame the idea of change as continuous improvement. This may help people face the reality that change is a normal component of organizational life. They may come to regard the normal state of their organizational and personal lives as being "permanent white water" (Vaill, 1992). A continuous-improvement perspective may help to create an orientation of "polishing the stone" rather than repairing a defect.

The concept of continuous improvement is reinforced by a systematic approach to managing change:

> Instead of viewing change as a mysterious event, we approach it as an understandable process that can be managed. This perspective allows people to avoid feeling victimized during transition; it promotes confidence that change can be planned and skillfully executed. (Conner, 1992, p. 7)

One approach to managing the change process is the P-D-C-A (Plan-Do-Check-Act) cycle (Senge et al., 1999), from the total quality management model. This approach provides a vehicle for carrying out the overall plan for a change effort, from initiation to implementation to institutionalization. In the "plan" phase, the organization collects and analyzes data, determines the vision and/or desired outcomes, and creates an initial plan and actions. In the "do" phase, the organization prepares people, builds the supportive environment, and implements the plan. The "check" phase is for examining results and methods. In the "act" phase, the organization takes appropriate actions to improve, maintain, or correct the plan and actions. Repeating this cycle results in a well-managed process and supports the concept of continuous improvement.

If change (a) is inevitable and (b) can be managed (as long as leaders remain flexible and in tune with the complexities and changing circumstances along the way), people are more likely to feel some degree of control instead of experiencing negative reactions, such as anger, confusion, or frustration. And if they believe that they possess some measure of control, they are more likely to support the change (Block, 1991).

▨ Reflection

What have you done (or can you do) to promote a broader view of change as a process of continuous improvement that can be managed? How are you helping all stakeholders engage in the process of continuous improvement?

▨ Notes

_____

_____

_____

_____

_____

_____

_____

_____

_____

▧ DAY 7: Complexity of Change

Change is a journey, not a blueprint.
—Michael Fullan

Change in all aspects of society, including education, now proceeds at a startling rate and with a complexity that is unknown in the history of civilization.

Daryl Conner (1993, p. 39) identifies seven factors that explain why change in today's world is so complex and rapid. They include the following:

- Faster communication and knowledge acquisition
- A growing world population
- Increasing interdependence and competition
- Limited resources
- Diversified political and religious ideologies
- Constant transitions of power
- Ecological distress

Most of these factors have their counterparts in the educational system: the rapid rate at which knowledge is changing, along with continuous improvements in information technology; the increase in the numbers of students from culturally diverse backgrounds; the growing awareness of the interrelatedness of schools and the communities in which they exist; the school voucher movement; tight resources; special interest groups; and the rapid turnover of superintendents. Each of these factors creates change independently of and in conjunction with the others.

Fullan (1993) describes an educational system that is trying to respond to this speed and complexity:

> School districts and schools are in the business of implementing a bewildering array of multiple innovations and policies simultaneously. Moreover, restructuring reforms are so multifaceted and complex that solutions for particular settings cannot be known in advance. If one tries to match the complexity of the situation with complex implementation plans, the process becomes unwieldy, cumbersome and usually wrong. (p. 24)

This illustrates why change must be regarded as a journey and not a blueprint. There are too many unknowns and unknowables; it may be impossible to determine the solution in advance. There are always unexpected events; rarely can they be fully predicted (that is why they're unexpected).

Change is a journey marked by detours, dead ends, and clover leafs, with an occasional stretch of clear motoring along the way. In extreme cases, even the original destination may be changed. This in no way obviates the need for an overall plan or the use of a process like the P-D-C-A cycle. You must recognize your destination as you near it. The repeated application of P-D-C-A will help you reach your target.

▨ Reflection

How are these seven factors relevant to the rate and complexity of change in your organization? Which are the most significant?

Think about some change effort or perhaps just a complex project that you have observed in your organization. Did things always go according to plan? For example:

- What events happened that were planned and accounted for in advance?

- What events happened that were unanticipated?

- Was the change effort or project flexible enough to handle the unexpected?

- Was it ultimately successful? If so, what factors contributed to its success?

- What lessons did the organization learn from the change? How was this understanding incorporated into subsequent efforts?

How can you help your organization better understand change as a journey that requires great flexibility and ongoing assessment?

▨ Notes

_____

_____

_____

_____

_____

_____

PART II

Listening to Individuals

Leaders of change initiatives must pay attention to people. Organizations don't change until the people in them change. That is why focusing on how people respond to a change initiative is so critical for success. Some related themes in these contemplations (Days 8–13) are that (a) response to a proposed change is highly individual, (b) the loss of the "old" needs to be grieved before people are able to fully embrace the "new," and (c) there are effective approaches people and organizations can use to prepare themselves for meeting the challenge of change initiatives with greater facility and comfort.

▨ DAY 8: Change as a People Process

Change does not occur until "someone" changes.
> —Susan Loucks-Horsley and Suzanne Stiegelbauer

It is very easy to refer to an organization as an entity separate from its people. We talk about how an organization fails to value individual initiative. Or we may discuss how resistant it is to change. We treat the institution as if it were a being in and of itself.

In reality, every organization is the sum total of the people who work there each day and the structures that organize them—policies, practices, and the culture. When we say that our organization fails to value individual initiative or is resistant to change, we are really talking about key individuals and/or the organizational policies, practices, or culture that these key individuals support.

That is why change fails in organizations unless we focus on people as well as on the change itself. Paying more attention to the change than to the people making the change dooms any initiative. "Since change is made by individuals, their personal satisfactions, frustrations, concerns, motivations, and perceptions all contribute to the success or failure of a change initiative" (Loucks-Horsley & Stiegelbauer, 1991).

▨ Reflection

Think of two or three times when you and your colleagues may have talked about your organization as if it were a separate entity apart from all who work there.

In these instances, what were you really referring to? Was it a specific person? Was it about some organizational policy or practice that you thought was unfair or outdated?

What might happen if, instead of crediting a separate identity to your organization, you more accurately pinpointed the people or aspects you had in mind?

▨ Notes

_____

_____

_____

▨ DAY 9: The Impact of Change

Whether people perceive a change as positive or negative depends not only on the actual outcomes of the change, but also on the degree of influence they believe they exert in the situation.
                                                        —Daryl Conner

Different people perceive change differently.

And the same change can affect people very differently. For some, the change may have little impact. For others, the impact may be great. Factors such as prior experience, level of knowledge and skill, individual resiliency, and the degree of influence a person has can affect how he or she experiences a change.

Here is an example. Which of the following would be hardest for you to do? Easiest?

- Move to a rural area?

- Relocate to midtown of a large city?

- Move to a foreign country?

- Sell your house to buy a different home in the same neighborhood?

All things being equal, most people would probably say that remaining in the same neighborhood would be easiest for them. But then, things are never equal when decisions about events such as those listed above must be made. Some people feel very comfortable moving to a rural area or to the heart of a major metropolis, especially if that is where they grew up. A military family that once lived in Japan might welcome a return. People's prior experiences greatly influence how they approach change. Usually, the greater the familiarity and comfort with a new situation, the greater the sense of control people feel.

If the impact of the change on individuals is small or slight, implementing the change is often a simple matter. For example, filling out a different time sheet or using a new procedure for ordering supplies are minor things for most people.

But if the change has a significant potential impact—especially if it affects people's self-confidence, their span of control, their comfort, or their competence—then expect resistance. With rare exceptions, it is human nature to resist anything that has a major impact on us—even something we really desire.

Recognize, too, that individual reactions to a change effort may in part be related to race, ethnicity, gender, disability, or life circumstances. For example, an organizational move may affect one ethnic or racial group more than another if the move is to an area where there are few members of their group.

Or if a change requires extensive professional development, sessions may need to be scheduled at different times to accommodate people with small children. As a leader, you must be alert to how different people are responding to a change initiative, which may or may not be readily apparent.

▨ Reflection

Think of a change effort in your organization, perhaps the same one you identified for Day 2. Think about how individuals responded to that change:

- Did some people implement the change with seemingly little effort? Were there any commonalties among these individuals?

- Did some people experience more difficulty? If so, did the change affect their confidence, control, comfort, and/or confidence?

- Did race, ethnicity, gender, disability, or life circumstances affect how people reacted to the change? If so, how?

Was the change successfully implemented or not? Why or why not? Can you relate success or failure to how different people responded to the change?

▨ Notes

_____

_____

_____

_____

_____

_____

▨ DAY 10: Moving Through the Stages of Change

*There is still and will always be a critical place for consideration
of the individual in the change process.*

—Susan Loucks-Horsley and Suzanne Stiegelbauer

The role of the individual in every organizational change effort is critical for its outcome. Everyone involved in a change has a somewhat different set of perceptions, expectations, feelings, motivations, and frustration points that are subject to change over time. These need to be addressed throughout the change process.

In general, we call these matters *concerns,* and these concerns are captured in CBAM (Hall & Hord, 2001). The CBAM details people's perceptions, feelings, and motivations in a way that enables change leaders to know, and even predict, what concerns people have and to respond appropriately.

The concerns model delineates seven stages that people move through as they implement a change (see Table 2.2). Response to the change is developmental in nature; and although people may differ in the pace at which they move through these stages, their concerns at each stage are similar.

Here are the stages and brief expressions of typical concerns (Hall & Hord, 2001):

Table 2.2 The Concerns-Based Adoption Model (CBAM): Stages of Concern

Stages	Expressions of Typical Concerns
VI: Refocusing	I have some ideas about something that would work even better.
V: Collaboration	How can I relate what I am doing to what others are doing?
IV: Consequence	How is my use affecting learners? How can I refine it to have more impact?
III: Management	I seem to be spending all my time getting materials ready.
II: Personal	How will using it affect me?
I: Informational	I would like to know more about it.
0: Awareness	I am not concerned about it.

SOURCE: From Hall & Hord, *Implementing Change: Patterns, Principles, and Potholes.*
Copyright © 2001 by Allyn & Bacon. Reprinted by permission.

The research on the model has revealed how people grow and develop through the stages. For example, individuals with limited experiences related to the change are likely to express concerns at Stages 0, I, or II (awareness, in-formational, or personal). As they become more involved, their concerns are likely to be at Stage III (management). As they gain confidence and start notic-ing their impact on learners, their concerns may move to Stage IV (conse-quences). With experience, their concerns may shift to wanting to collaborate (Stage V) or searching for better approaches (Stage VI). Levels 0, I, and II are concerns that are focused on *self;* Level III is focused on *task;* and Levels IV, V, and VI are concerns about *impact.*

Thus, the model predicts the development of individuals within a group and enables us to assess where a group is at any moment. Knowing where peo-ple are enables the leaders of any change effort to target their interventions more effectively. For example, there is no point in focusing on management issues when the group isn't even familiar enough with the proposed change to identify what management issues they might encounter.

▨ Reflection

Think about a change initiative in your organization.

Are you aware of the different concerns people have? Do they encompass the entire continuum listed above, or are they concentrated in the self, task, or impact levels?

How can the information about the CBAM help you in leading your change effort?

▨ Notes

_____

_____

_____

_____

_____

_____

▨ DAY 11: Accepting Loss

He that lacks time to mourn lacks time to mend.

—William Shakespeare

In some way, all significant change involves giving up something of your former self, and all losses must be grieved.

Whenever a major change takes place, we lose something. It may be the loss of a relationship, an office, or a lesson we loved to teach. Even if we want the change (perhaps a better relationship, a nicer office, or an improved curriculum), we will still feel a loss. The loss may be a pattern of interaction, a convenient working environment, or the joy of helping others learn something important to us; or it may be the loss of that which was comfortable and familiar.

A loss that remains ungrieved keeps us anchored in the past, unable to fully commit to the present. From the work of Dr. Elisabeth Kübler-Ross (1970), we learn something about how people grieve death. She has identified five stages of the grief process:

Stage 1: *Denial.* We pretend that nothing has happened. Things will be just the way they have always been. Perhaps we are having a bad dream. We'll wake up, and everything will be fine. We may enter into a robot-like stage in which we suppress our anger and become depressed. Because we are in denial, we don't tell other people. In fact, we haven't even told ourselves.

Stage 2: *Anger.* Feeling angry about a loss is normal and necessary. We may feel angry at another person, maybe even at the world. Why did this have to happen to us? Life isn't fair. Or: Why did this have to happen now? The timing is not good.

Stage 3: *Bargaining.* In this stage, we seek to make amends. What do we have to do to restore conditions to what they were? What can we trade or give up? What can we promise to do or never do again?

Stage 4: *Letting go.* This stage is the final letting go of the old. It is, in one sense, the darkness before the dawn. It may be characterized by deep sadness. It is a reflective stage in that we ask deep questions, such as "What is the meaning of this experience?" "What do I truly want for myself?" "What have I learned over the past weeks or months?" Rarely does letting go occur at a single instant. Rather, it occurs incrementally.

Stage 5: *Acceptance.* Here, we have moved beyond our emotional attachment to the loss and have relinquished our investment in the past. We are now ready to move and to accept whatever new situation is awaiting. We are reenergized and hopeful about the future.

Movement through the stages is similar to that of an organization going through systemic reform. Progress is not linear, and it is possible for people to become stuck in a stage or skip a stage completely. Some may even work backward or appear to move in circles. However, for the grieving process to be most effective, grievers need—at some point—to experience each stage.

In organizations, resistance may come from losses ungrieved. According to Garmston and Wellman (1999), "Endings must be marked concretely and symbolically" (p. 248). In the absence of grieving, the staff may hold on to elements of the old and not be able to fully embrace the new.

▨ Reflection

Again, think of a major change going on in your organization. What is the loss that the staff may be feeling? Have you found ways to help people grieve that loss? If so, how? If not, what steps can you take to facilitate the process of natural grieving?

▨ Notes

_____

_____

_____

_____

_____

_____

_____

_____

▨ DAY 12: Change and Resilience

Become consciously competent about your own resilience.

—Daryl Conner

How well equipped are people to handle change? How do you know their potential for responding to change?

Daryl Conner (1998) sees each person as having an individual speed of change. He defines this as

> the rate at which you can move through the adaptation process with a minimum of dysfunctional behavior—the pace at which you can bounce back from the confusion caused by uncertainty and grasp the opportunities that the new environment presents. (p. 189)

According to Conner, the single, most important factor that affects one's speed of change is resilience. Highly resilient individuals are able to operate at a higher speed of change than those who are less resilient.

Conner (1998, p. 189) has identified five characteristics that constitute resiliency:

1. *Positiveness:* Resilient individuals effectively identify opportunities in turbulent environments and have confidence in their ability to succeed.

2. *Focus:* Resilient individuals have a clear vision of what they want to achieve, and they use this as a lodestar to guide them should they become disoriented.

3. *Flexibility:* Resilient individuals draw effectively on a wide range of internal and external resources to develop creative, malleable strategies for responding to change.

4. *Organization:* Resilient individuals use structured approaches to manage ambiguity, planning, and coordinating effectively in implementing their strategies.

5. *Proactivity:* Resilient individuals act in the face of uncertainty and take calculated risks rather than seeking comfort.

Although these five factors are interrelated to some extent, they are separate attributes. One change may draw principally from one or two factors, whereas another change may tap a different factor. This led Conner (1998) to view resilience as "the ability to draw effectively on whichever characteristic, or combination of characteristics, is called for in a particular situation" (p. 193).

Conner (1998) also sees a link between resiliency and physical health. The higher the resiliency, the greater the likelihood of excellent physical health and vice versa. He has also identified a similar link between the level of resilience and leadership. Leaders in organizations are more likely to have higher levels of resilience, and those with high resilience are more likely to be leaders.

▨ Reflection

Using Conner's five factors (positiveness, focus, flexibility, organization, and proactivity) plus overall physical health, how would you rate the resiliency of key individuals involved in your change effort? Which of these factors stand out? How are they manifested?

Although resiliency is personal, it can be affected by what goes on in an organization. As a leader, what can you do to bolster people's positiveness, focus, flexibility, organization, proactivity, and overall physical health?

▨ Notes

_____

_____

_____

_____

_____

_____

_____

▨ DAY 13: Embracing Problems

Problems are our friends.

—Michael Fullan

Sounds a little scary, right? This is especially true given the complex nature of the problems that organizations and society as a whole face today. How can problems have any kind of positive connotation?

Problems in the broadest sense are inevitable. Given the increasing complexity of our society and the rapid rate of change, we are going to experience more and more problems, most of which will be complex and not easily resolved. It is our reality—whether we like it or not. If we confront our fears, we have a better chance of resolving them. Rather than trying to avoid a problem or pretend it doesn't exist, we are better off facing it directly.

It is through solving problems, often by trial and error, that we learn. As the saying goes, "No pain, no gain!" Without the problem, we would not have the learning. One of the characteristics of adaptive organizations is an acceptance of failure as inevitable and valuable. We often learn more from a failed attempt than a successful one. In today's organizations, however, failure is not carte blanche. It is balanced with accountability. What Garmston and Wellman (1999) call *failing forward* is the way people learn from their errors.

▨ Reflection

What is the prevailing attitude in your organization toward problems? Are they ignored? Seen as troublesome interruptions? Looked on as opportunities to improve products or services and to advance knowledge in the organization?

What is your organization's attitude toward failure? Are people able and willing to take risks without fear of recrimination? Do people learn from their mistakes, and does that learning become part of the organization's common knowledge?

As a leader, what can you do (a) to help people in your organization see problems as friends rather than enemies and (b) to establish a climate supportive of failing forward?

▨ Notes

PART III
Responsibilities in Directing Change

A successful organization must lead change. Although change is inevitable, it is possible to anticipate and intentionally direct a wide range of organizational changes. This is the leader's role: to know what specific changes the organization is facing and ensure that the appropriate conditions are in place to support the change.

The contemplations in this section focus on the leader's role in directing and guiding change. In carrying out their responsibilities, leaders model the effective practices they are seeking to implement. For example, they guide development of personal and organizational visions and their accompanying missions. Through understanding how people change, they build commitment among the staff as well as other key stakeholders. They address the conditions for change, making sure that others have what they need—be it knowledge, skills, changes in the environment, or resources. They empower others to assume greater responsibility. Although change is a collaborative undertaking, single leaders can accomplish a great deal merely by modeling appropriate and inspiring behavior. Effective leaders of change also need to know how they themselves are reacting to the change prior to leading others.

▨ DAY 14: Motivating Others

There is only one way under high Heaven to get anybody to do anything. Did you ever stop to think of that? Yes, just one way. And that is by making the other person want to do it. Remember, there is no other way.

—Dale Carnegie

What is motivation to change? Is it simple or complex, one-dimensional or multidimensional?

What sustains motivation to achieve a goal? What keeps us going even when our chances of success seem remote?

According to Richard Barrett (1999), motivation has four dimensions: physical, emotional, mental, and spiritual. The physical and emotional dimensions are satisfied primarily by external conditions. For example, financial reward is an example of the physical component; open communication is an example of the emotional. Physical and emotional aspects can be fulfilled by either positive external incentives (e.g., promotions) or negative external incentives (e.g., loss of status). The efficiency of external rewards declines over time and so must be increased to remain motivational.

Although individuals will be motivated by all four dimensions, the most sustainable level of commitment comes when mental and spiritual needs are satisfied. The mental dimension is met through opportunities for professional and personal growth or opportunities to use new knowledge and skills to solve real problems. The spiritual dimension is met through having work that is meaningful, work that matters, and work that makes a difference in the world.

Commitments are sustained by *creative tension* (Fritz, 1989). Think of a stretched rubber band. One pole is your current reality: the existing state you are dissatisfied with, the state causing you to feel discomfort. The other pole is your vision: that which you want to achieve. The discrepancy between the poles creates a tension, and the natural resolution of tension is to move closer to the vision of what you want (Senge et al., 1999). If this tension is strong enough, individuals may feel compelled to persevere because "they have assimilated the vision not just consciously, but unconsciously, at a level where it changes more of their behavior." They may have a "sustained sense of energy and enthusiasm, which . . . produces some tangible results, which can then make the energy and enthusiasm stronger" (Senge, Roberts, Ross, Smith, & Kleiner, 1994, p. 195).

Reaching this level of commitment generally suggests that people have satisfied the mental and spiritual dimensions of their motivation. If not, the tension would be inadequate to support sustained action.

▧ Reflection

Think about the reform effort you lead. What dimensions of motivation are most commonly addressed? Are there incentives and disincentives for people's physical and emotional needs? What opportunities exist for fulfilling the mental and spiritual needs? Is there professional development, and can people solve problems using this new knowledge and skill? Do they find the work meaningful? Do they have a sense of making a difference? If the rewards are more external than internal, what can you as a leader do to address the mental and spiritual aspects and strengthen commitment?

Consider the people involved in your change effort. On a scale of 1 (low) to 10 (high), how much tension do they experience between your organization's current reality and your desired state? What evidence do you have to make this determination? How do you either maintain or increase that tension? Are there any additional strategies that might enhance people's commitment to reform?

▧ Notes

_____

_____

_____

_____

_____

_____

_____

▨ DAY 15: Origins of Change

To affect true change, one must become a leader of leaders, one who inspires others to lead the transformation.

—James O'Toole

How many times have you heard people (maybe even yourself) debating about whether organizational change comes from the top or the bottom and where it should actually originate?

A typical conversation may sound something like this. "You can't impose change from the top. I don't care how many edicts leaders issue, change can't be mandated. If the people don't want to change, there are all kinds of ways to undermine any initiative. Any real change has to come from the staff—not the leaders. Let me tell you about what happened in my organization. . . ."

Another counters: "People at lower levels rarely have the power, authority, or resources to bring about any kind of major change on their own. Quit kidding yourself. Organizations can squelch a budding initiative just by firing a person or two or denying them resources. Any real change has to have the sanctions and support of leaders. Let me tell you about what happened in my organization. . . ."

And so the arguments go. If you have found yourself caught up in such discussions, vow right now that you won't repeat such a conversation. The question itself is a spurious one, posed as either/or: Change comes either from the top or from the bottom.

In reality, it is both. Both the leaders and the staff must be active players in a change initiative if it is to succeed. Either one is capable of subverting a change, so both must be working in concert to ensure success.

▨ Reflection

Think of some change effort in your organization that succeeded. What role did the leaders play? What was the staff's role? How was the change initiated? Was it lodged more in the top or the base of the organization, or was it spread across the organization? Did the leaders support the change effort? (Many change efforts fail because leaders don't provide sustained support.)

How did the staff come to implement the change effort? (Change efforts can also fail because the staff does not have the knowledge and skills to carry out the new initiative.) How were people informed? Did the change effort expand to include more people? How did this happen? What can you learn from this effort that would help you in your role of leading change?

▨ Notes

_____

_____

_____

_____

_____

_____

_____

_____

_____

_____

_____

▨ DAY 16: Balancing Constants and Change

*The art of progress is to preserve order amid change
and to preserve change amid order.*

—Alfred North Whitehead

Change, change, change! We hear that word so much these days. So much, in fact, that we may forget that change is just one pole in one of the fundamental dichotomies of life. The other choice is to stay the same.

In many change efforts, the parts that stay the same are overlooked. The entire focus is on the change(s) going on—not the elements that remain stable, stationary, and strong in the midst of change.

Dichotomies (centralization versus decentralization, holding on versus letting go, and staying the same versus changing) are best viewed as "both/ ands" rather than "either/ors."

In any successful change effort, considerable attention needs to be given to what remains constant. Without this balanced view, the daunting perception of change can overwhelm a system and the people in it.

So, how do you balance staying the same and changing in an organization? You deliberately and thoughtfully designate some things that will not change during a certain period. For example, your school will implement a new curriculum in mathematics and science for K-6 over the next three years, but the reading and social studies curricula will remain the same. Or when your organization is merging with another, elements that each keeps for itself and what each gives up in the merger are clearly specified.

Balance can also be achieved by conducting a change priority inventory (Kaser & Horsley, 1998a) so that competing change initiatives do not negate each other in their struggle for resources. Such an inventory can identify what is not being changed, along with the changes that are slated to take place.

The areas of stability need to be highlighted in written and oral communications and supported by leaders in the organization. This assures that the staff knows that the leadership is committed to balanced change and to keeping what is good and what works well within the organization.

▨ Reflection

Jot down some of the change initiatives going on in your workplace. Can you balance each change effort with some parallel aspect of your organization that is remaining stable? If you can't, people are likely to feel overwhelmed by all the changes.

If your organization is not emphasizing stability sufficiently to balance the desired change, what can you do?

▨ Notes

▨ DAY 17: Applying Personal Mastery

Successful individuals and successful businesses have one thing in common: They share the power of purpose. The more we focus on achieving a desired outcome, the greater the likelihood of success.

—Richard Barrett

What does it take for an organization to become adept at responding to change?

One requirement is what Peter Senge (1990) calls *personal mastery*. Personal mastery is the discipline of personal growth and learning. There are three characteristics of personal mastery: a strong sense of personal vision, a commitment to learning to see reality more clearly, and the ability to clarify continually what is most important to us.

When Senge uses the term *vision*, he means a specific picture of what people want for their organizations and themselves. A vision is more than just a picture; it is a picture to which one is passionately committed.

Seeing reality more clearly involves a commitment to telling the truth, especially to ourselves. It seems to be a common characteristic for people to deny that problems exist in their organizations or their personal lives and that there is any need to change. Perhaps we think there is no solution to a problem; perhaps others will be upset if we surface the problem; perhaps we are afraid that we will be blamed; or we think it is someone else's job to deal with this problem. For whatever reason, we find it very easy and comfortable to deny what really exists. A commitment to telling the truth makes denial much more difficult.

A key component of managing change is knowing the conditions that exist at a given time: what the change will be and how wide the gap is between current conditions and the ideal state. This requires a leader to be skilled in and committed to personal mastery.

How often do you find yourself wondering what you are doing or what your organization is doing, and why? Those committed to personal mastery regularly ask themselves these questions. It is so easy to get caught up in things that really don't matter to us or are not important—and not attend to what is central to our lives. Our attention to what is unimportant compromises our commitment to what we really want and slows or thwarts the change process.

▨ Reflection

Think of some examples of how you model personal mastery in your organization.

Do you have a personal vision for your role within your organization? Do you share that with others?

What is your commitment to telling the truth about what is happening in your organization? Do you ever find yourself denying reality rather than addressing problems head on? What are the things that don't get talked about in your organization? How can you surface these issues with people who need to address them?

How often do you ask yourself what you are doing and why? How well are you able to stay on track with what is truly important to you and your organization?

To what extent are your colleagues committed to personal mastery? What can you do as a leader to model a climate of personal mastery in your organization?

▨ Notes

▨ DAY 18: Recognizing Mental Models

The inertia of deeply entrenched mental models can overwhelm even the best systemic insights.

—Peter Senge

A second requirement for an organization to respond successfully to change is awareness of what Senge (1990) calls *mental models*. Mental models run the gamut from simple generalizations or stereotypes about people and things to complex belief systems about how the world works. Senge believes that these mental models influence how we think and act.

One common example of a firmly entrenched mental model is how educators have viewed teaching and learning over the years. Historically, they have looked upon teaching as the act of transmitting information to students who did not have it. Students were viewed as largely passive learners directed by teachers who knew more than they did. Now this view is changing. Instead, we regard students as active and as possessing knowledge, and thus nearly all aspects of education are subject to question. As Isaacson and Bamburg (1992) point out, we now have the opportunity to question "Assumptions about children, learning, instructional strategies, curriculums, relationships with parents, and the school calendar and schedule—even furniture and architecture" (p. 43).

Another mental model being challenged by contemporary thought is that of leadership. Rather than leadership being vested only in the midlevel and top management of an organization (the firmly entrenched model again), we are now regarding all staff as having certain leadership responsibilities. But if that is the case, we have to set up some different structures in our organizations to accommodate, support, and encourage this broader concept of leadership. Old structures don't mesh with the new mental model.

We act on the basis of our mental models continually, so it is important to be aware of what they are. When we decide, we act on our assumptions; and the assumptions usually remain implicit. Making our assumptions or mental models explicit helps us communicate better and can lead to more effective decision making and problem solving.

▨ Reflection

Can you identify some of the basic mental models you and other individuals in your organization hold? Perhaps start with views of leadership. What are the assumptions you and others hold about who should be a leader and what traits leaders should possess?

What are some of the mental models you and others hold about your organization? Do you assume all can succeed, or do you think some must fail? Do you believe that individuals must have certain prerequisites or follow a certain path to be successful? Do you think you know more about what you do than your customers do? Do you view your organization as impervious to change? What could happen if you changed your mental models? How might changing a mental model affect the outcome of a change initiative?

▨ Notes

_____

_____

_____

_____

_____

_____

_____

_____

_____

▧ DAY 19: Shared Vision

The very essence of leadership is [that] you have to have a vision.
It's got to be a vision you articulate clearly and forcefully on
every occasion. You can't blow an uncertain trumpet.
　　　　　　　　　　　　　　　—Father Theodore Hesburgh

Shared vision, another critical component of organizational change, doesn't emerge from a small group effort or by upper-level managers issuing a statement that others are expected to follow. A true vision is never imposed. It evolves through people having a similar picture of what they want and knowing that they can achieve this goal most effectively by their collective, not individual, actions.

A shared vision is synergistic. It drives action within an organization, which in turn, drives results. For people who truly care about something, the tasks, however onerous, are simply the means for attaining their common goals. A vision is dynamic, evolving. It may change with circumstances over time.

Reaching shared vision starts with individuals crafting their personal visions. "If people don't have their own vision, all they can do is 'sign up' for someone else's" (Senge, 1990, p. 211). Senge points out that the result is compliance rather than commitment. It is the personal vision that motivates. People with their own personal visions can form a powerful group to create what they want for themselves and for their organization.

A litmus test of the power of a vision is whether people know it and can articulate it clearly. A vision fails the test when it is merely something on a piece of paper that has to be looked up.

A leader's role is to help people develop their own personal visions and map those onto a vision for the organization that drives individual and collective action.

▧ Reflection

Consider a change initiative in your organization that you are involved with. Does it have a compelling vision? Do people have personal visions that are aligned with the broader vision?

As a leader, what will you do with others to develop personal and organizational visions? How can having a sense of personal mastery and an awareness of your own mental models help you in vision building?

▨ Notes

▨ DAY 20: Missions and Goals

*The greatest satisfaction you can find in life comes from
discovering and courageously following your mission.*

—Richard Barrett

What gives an organization a common sense of direction?

As the previous contemplation points out, a shared vision is absolutely essential for any change initiative to succeed. However, more is required.

Organizations need to be clear about their mission—who they are and what their purpose is and how this relates to the change effort. This is different from a vision that describes the future state or conditions an organization desires. There may also be more specific goals suggesting activities or programs appropriate to the mission that will help achieve the shared vision.

Although there is usually just one shared vision, different parts of an organization may have their own mission statements and goals that are aligned with the shared vision. In some organizations, individuals write personal mission statements that are compatible with their unit's. This results in a staff that has a common sense of direction.

For leaders, having a shared vision, clear mission, and specific goals are essential parts of change management. Together, these items serve as a compass for organizational action. Top-down, autocratic management is inappropriate for the "Information Age." Today, most workers require a high level of autonomy to perform their work properly. In the absence of tight controls, a common sense of direction enables individuals to work toward the common good rather than focusing only on their piece of the whole.

▨ Reflection

As a leader of change, how do you communicate with others about the shared vision and the reform effort's mission and goals? Are there different missions and goals for different parts of your organization? If so, are they aligned with the vision? Are you clear about your own mission and goals? What would other staff members say about the organization's vision and mission?

What can you do to gain greater clarity of vision, mission, and goals for yourself and others, if that is needed?

▨ Notes

_____

_____

_____

_____

_____

_____

_____

_____

_____

_____

_____

_____

▨ DAY 21: Tackling Resistance

One cannot hope to implement change without persuading people that it is necessary. This is a task of daunting proportions that must often start by challenging people's view of themselves, their performance and their clients.

—Robert Evans

Getting people to feel some sense of urgency for a major change is an art form. Lowering resistance is a balancing act. It involves increasing the tension of not supporting the change effort and reducing the tension related to trying it. Both drive behavior in the direction of the change.

What are some ways of decreasing resistance to change?

Increase the tension of not supporting the change
- Provide data that documents the need for the change.
- Make it clear that all are expected to make the change.
- Make sure that key opinion leaders at each unit of the organization support and model the change. Have them garner the support of others.

Decrease the tension related to trying the new way
- Determine the concerns of the resisters. Respond with the appropriate intervention.
- Help resisters make the connection between their personal visions and the organizational vision.
- Set up a timetable that allows adequate assimilation time.

In describing what often happens in organizations, John Kotter (1996) says,

> I've seen people start by building the change coalitions, by creating the change vision, or by simply making changes. But the problems of inertia and complacency always seem to catch up with them. Sometimes they quickly hit a wall, as when a lack of urgency makes it impossible to put together a powerful enough leadership team to guide the changes. Sometimes people go for years before it becomes apparent that various initiatives are flagging. (p. 49)

One way that leaders keep people out of the "complacency zone" is to identify and celebrate milestones in the implementation of the change effort. This helps people know where they are and keeps attention and energy focused on the success of the change effort. It also gives people a sense of control and accomplishment.

One caution: If the degree or extent of resistance seems greater than would normally be expected, leaders should look at the change initiative itself. Perhaps it is not the appropriate initiative for the time or circumstances. Maybe there is a better solution waiting. Knowing people's specific objections can help you determine if you need to reconsider what you are proposing.

▨ Reflection

As a leader of change, what do you do when people resist change? Have your strategies focused both on decreasing disincentives and increasing incentives? If your change requires a long time for implementation, is there a danger of people becoming complacent? If so, how can you keep people engaged and reduce complacency?

▨ Notes

_____

_____

_____

_____

_____

_____

_____

▧ DAY 22: Establishing Stakeholder Information Systems

Unless you regularly account for all your stakeholders, your organization will likely not survive.

—Stephen Covey

Who is involved in your reform effort?

If your organization is a private one, change may be somewhat easier because you are likely to have fewer stakeholders. If your organization is public, your group of stakeholders is broader. In addition to your employees and governing body, you may have unions, children and youth, parents and community members, businesses, other institutions, and perhaps even some special interest groups to which you must attend.

Implementing any kind of lasting change is so difficult that you may want to limit involvement. However, ignoring some group or not keeping key people properly informed is likely to backfire and may derail your initiative later. If you only occasionally reach out to stakeholders, you are likely to raise stakeholders' expectations and have them experience frustration if their involvement does not lead to change.

Covey (1992) points out that real change happens when organizations begin to problem solve around data gained from stakeholders. He recommends a "stakeholder information system—a feedback system or database on what shareholders, customers, employees, communities, suppliers, distributors, and other parties want and expect" (Covey, 1992, p. 258). He suggests that if a stakeholder information system is set up properly, data can be highly accurate as long as they are obtained "systematically, scientifically, anonymously, using random sampling of the population" (Covey, 1992, p. 258).

Here is an instance of a school administrator who failed to consider his stakeholders: His elementary school was slated to be closed, and students would be moved to a much larger, more modern school across town. He went on record as fully supporting this decision. The school they were leaving was old, lacked a gym and adequate wiring for computers, and was not handicapped accessible. The parents were outraged. They saw the smallness and character of the old school, the individual attention it afforded children, and its proximity and community school atmosphere as benefits that far outweighed the negatives. In a public forum, the principal was shown to be out of touch with one of his most important stakeholder groups.

Using Covey's idea of establishing a stakeholder information system, how could this situation have been avoided?

▨ Reflection

Who are the stakeholders affected by the change your organization is proposing? What assumptions are you making about how they will react to the change? Have you verified your assumptions with members of the group?

How are you involving them in your reform effort? Has anyone been left out? If so, why? How will you bring them on board?

Do you have a stakeholder information system established? If not, how could you establish one?

▨ Notes

_____

_____

_____

_____

_____

_____

_____

_____

_____

▨ DAY 23: Managing Multiple Change Efforts

Q: How can executives manage 29 change projects all at once?

A: They can't. In successful transformations, executives lead the overall effort and leave most of the managerial work and the leadership of specific activities to their subordinates.

—John P. Kotter

The nomenclature used in this section of the book (i.e., the use of the terms that describe reform efforts or change initiatives) may be misleading. Expressions such as *developing a mission* or *data-based decision making* may lead a reader to believe that change occurs in a linear fashion, one initiative at a time.

Nothing, however, could be farther from the truth. It would be rare for an organization to have a single reform effort in place. It is not uncommon for a school district, for example, to identify 50 or more changes going on at the district level and even more in individual schools.

One of the major reasons reform efforts fail is that they are overrun by others that have more support and resources. Unless upper management attends specifically to each reform effort and its relationship to the vision, mission, and goals of the organization, some inevitably kill off others. *Attending* means (a) knowing what resources each reform effort needs to be successful and delivering it and/or (b) prioritizing the various change efforts so that each has a different ranking over a specific period of time. Such determinations cannot be haphazard.

Attending to each change effort independently is critical for another reason. Each has its own vision, mission, and goals; its own assumptions; and its own staffing. Sponsors and supporters, including stakeholders, are likely to be different. The impact of the change varies from one initiative to another; and it is the impact of change on people that determines how easy or difficult implementation will be. If you are gathering data about your reform effort, they must be collected separately for each initiative.

Just as you need to treat each change initiative individually, you need to see each in relation to the others and support appropriate coordination and integration. A major organizational paradox exists: treating each change effort individually while seeing each as part of a larger whole. As a leader, you need to keep the big picture in mind, looking across the different initiatives to note overlap and meeting coordination and integration needs.

▨ Reflection

Make a list of the changes going on in your organization. (You might ask a colleague to do the same thing and then compare your lists.) How many did you come up with? Were you surprised by the number? Why?

Do any of these change efforts compete with each other for resources? Are any in danger of failing? If so, what can you do to salvage change initiatives that are threatened?

Is each change effort being treated independently and at the same time being seen as part of a larger whole? If not, what can you do to make sure that each change initiative is seen from this dual perspective? Can you identify linkages between and among the various change efforts?

Are the change efforts aligned with the organization's vision, mission, and goals and with each other?

▨ Notes

_____

_____

_____

_____

_____

_____

_____

_____

▨ DAY 24: Capitalizing on Resistance

Understand that resistance can be a gold mine!

—Carol Bershad and Susan Mundry

When you hear the word *resistance,* does it conjure up a positive or a negative reaction?

Most people will think negatively: that resistance is an obstacle and something to be overcome.

What would happen if you reframed the notion of resistance? What if you saw it as an indicator of where people were in relation to a change? What if you saw resistance as an opportunity for you and others to learn? How might this change your perspective?

The level of resistance to change in an organization often gives us insight into the potential impact of the change. The greater the impact of the change, the more resistance it is likely to encounter. For example, substituting one textbook for another is not likely to have great impact and therefore, minimal resistance is likely to appear. However, moving from a textbook to an activity-based curriculum is likely to have much greater impact and therefore, give rise to greater resistance. Resistance is normal and natural. If there is no resistance, you can assume that the impact of change is minimal or that people are indifferent.

Understanding that resistance stems from feelings can help us delve deeper to determine the source of resistance. And once we know the source of the resistance, dealing with it becomes much easier. Here are 12 common sources of resistance divided into different categories (Kaser & Horsley, 1998b, pp. 1-2):

Sources related to not having the ability to change
- Lack of knowledge and skills in the content
- Lack of knowledge and skills in the process

Sources related to the lack of willingness to change
- Lack of support for the change because of poor communication
- Lack of ownership, seeing no need
- Lack of alignment between the change and the culture of the organization
- Lack of resources of time, materials, and/or facilities
- Having an oppositional nature (either individuals or a group); disliking the mandated change
- Lack of leadership or positive role models
- Lack of trust in the system or in the leaders

Sources related to special circumstances
- Giving the appearance of resisting change (but not actually doing so) because of style differences with those leading the change
- Having a sincere and accurate belief that the proposed change is wrong or that it is being implemented the wrong way
- Personal reasons unrelated to the change (e.g., focusing on another challenging work project or change effort, impending retirement, pregnancy, serious illness, etc.)

▨ Reflection

How much resistance do you encounter for your current change effort? Can you identify the sources of the resistance? What steps are you taking to overcome the resistance? What can other people do?

Can you think of at least one antidote for each one of the 12 sources of resistance? There are actually several for each one of the sources, so if you can come up with more than one, you are thinking in the right direction.

How can you use the sources of resistance in leading your reform effort?

▨ Notes

_____

_____

_____

_____

_____

_____

▨ DAY 25: Empowering Others

Empowerment is the creation of an environment in which employees at all levels feel that they have real influence over standards of quality, service, and business effectiveness within their areas of responsibility.

—Price Waterhouse Change Integration Team

"Oh, no. Not *empowerment!* I'm so sick of hearing this word. Empowering has become a cliché. I'm not even sure what the word means anymore."

Have you heard this before? Although empowerment has been used somewhat indiscriminately, the basic concept of helping people become more powerful and take greater control of and responsibility for all aspects of their lives is an important institutional characteristic.

Major changes must involve people at all levels of an organization. If people feel powerless and that they have little or no control, they are not likely to support or implement a change.

How do you help people feel and become powerful? Here are four steps to enable people to feel more in control of what is happening to them (Kotter, 1996):

- Include them in the visioning process and make sure that they are supported for having their own personal visions.

- Make sure that organizational infrastructures are aligned with the vision.

- Provide skills and/or attitude training that people need to do their jobs, including follow-up support.

- Confront and work with any leaders who don't support the change.

▨ Reflection

What experiences have you had in empowering others? What strategies worked best? What attempts were dead ends?

Consider those people involved in your organization's change effort. On a scale of 1(low) to 10 (high), how powerful do you think they feel? Are there ways you can increase their sense of control, level of responsibility, and ability to take action?

▨ Notes

▨ DAY 26: Modeling Behavior

I decide. I do. Me.

—Frank Hague

What can a single person do?

So much of this chapter stresses that change is a collaborative effort. It is highly unlikely that a single individual can carry out a major change initiative. Organizations are far too complex for one person to exert that degree of influence.

Does that mean there is nothing an individual person can accomplish? Not at all. As a leader, you can serve as a catalyst for change and in that process, serve as a model for others.

At minimum, here is what you can do:

- Commit yourself to personal mastery. Decide to be the best you can be and pursue a path to high performance.

- Dedicate yourself to being a continual learner and to see problems as opportunities for learning and change.

- Acknowledge your failures and stress what you have learned.

- Willingly share your knowledge and resources with others who are interested in what you are doing.

- Organize and convene teams to address problems and suggest improvements.

- Offer to coach others.

- Use data for your decision making, and let others know what use you make of this information.

- Be able to articulate your vision, mission, and goals clearly and concisely.

- Actively support change efforts you believe in.

Essentially, you are modeling the attitudes and behaviors that are supportive of systemic reform. Moreover, you are taking on a leadership role, even though your position may or may not be one of institutional leadership. If you do these things in a way that is respectful of your colleagues and the organization as a whole, you will make a difference. In fact, you may be the catalyst for starting a major change effort or implementing one.

▨ Reflection

How do you see yourself functioning in your organization? As a single person, are you having all the influence that you possibly can? On a scale of

1 (low) to 10 (high), where do you rate yourself on influence? Are there ways you can be more influential?

Of the list above, which of the following are you doing now? Which could you do? What would be the likely result?

▨ Notes

_____

_____

_____

_____

_____

_____

_____

_____

_____

_____

▨ DAY 27: Self-Assessment as a Change Leader

An ounce of practice is worth more than tons of preaching.
—Mahatma Gandhi

This section focuses on what leaders must do to lead successful change initiatives in their organizations. Therefore, the questions in the reflections are designed to stimulate thinking about the leader's role in the organization in relation to the topic of the contemplation.

However, leaders increase their credibility and their likelihood for success if they have experienced what they expect others to do. It is very important for leaders of change to go through major change initiatives themselves. They need to experience resistance firsthand and work through it so they can help others do the same. They need to understand and be committed to personal mastery and exhibit behavior congruent with its principles.

As a leader, you convey what you think and feel more by your actions than by your words. Your colleagues judge you more by what you do than by what you say. Therefore, you need to assess your own personal experience base in dealing with change as part of expanding your leadership role.

▨ Reflection

Here is a list of questions for you to consider as part of your expanding ability to lead change in your organization. They are intended to get you started on your self-assessment.

- Think of two or three changes you have experienced—either personal or professional. What was the impact of the changes on you? Was their impact similar for your colleagues? If the changes had a differential impact, what do you attribute that to?

- When you are experiencing a change, what needs to remain stable in your life? How much change can you handle? How do you know your limit?

- Have you had the experience of grieving for losses when a change has taken place? If so, how have you done that? What works best for you?

- What is your commitment to personal mastery? Do you have a personal vision for your work and personal life? Do you view yourself as a lifelong learner? Why or why not? Are you committed to telling the truth about your current reality? Can you recall instances in which you have denied the truth about what was currently happening?

- Think of some recent decisions or actions you took at home or at work. Can you identify at least five mental models that influenced what you did? What assumptions were you making? Did you share these with others so they understood your decision or action better? Are the underlying assumptions you operated with the ones you want? What could you do to change a mental model that no longer works for you?

- How do you use data in your work and life? What are your most reliable sources of information? Are they diverse enough? Can you recall instances in which you ignored data? What were the consequences?

- What is your typical reaction when you discover some problem that you need to address? How might you respond if you regarded a new problem as an opportunity for learning?

- What visions do you have for your professional work? How committed are you to this vision? What would make you more committed to it? Who has a similar vision, or do you hold these visions alone? Is your mission in line with your vision? If not, what do you need to do to make it more so?

- Do you have plans for achieving any of the visions you hold? What is your plan?

- What is the speed at which you respond to change? How do you assess your speed in relation to the speed of other people? How resilient are you? What would make you more resilient?

Based on your answers to these questions, how comfortable do you feel in leading a major change initiative? What could increase your level of comfort? What kind of experiences are you lacking? How can you get the experience you need?

▨ Notes

_____

_____

_____

_____

PART IV

Paying Attention to the Organization

Pay attention to the organization as well as the people. Although paying attention to the people is paramount in any change initiative, change leaders must be mindful of impact to the organization. Without this broader view, no change initiative can be successful.

The last set of contemplations (Days 28–31) in this part focus specifically on organizations. There are some key aspects of systems thinking that are important for anyone leading a change effort. Determining an organization's character (or personality) can help the leaders select effective change strategies. The organization's history of making change influences how any current initiative is received and is usually an accurate predictor of success. Finally, a leader can assess his or her organization's readiness to take on a major change effort.

▧ DAY 28: Systems Thinking

In a messy world, systems thinking is essential.

—Robert Garmston and Bruce Wellman

What is systems thinking, and how does it relate to organizational change?

Systems thinking is a particular way of looking at organizational behavior. It is a *body of knowledge and tools* that helps identify underlying patterns and suggests how they can be changed.

In his book *The Fifth Discipline,* Peter Senge (1990) outlines 11 "laws" that are characteristic of systems thinking. Three of these are especially relevant to bringing about change in organizations.

"Today's problems come from yesterday's 'solutions'" (p. 57). Although we usually hope that solving a problem takes care of a situation, in reality, solving one problem often creates another. For example, the high school that instituted a high minimum grade point average for all athletes found that its dropout rate increased. Instead of motivating students to study harder and get good grades, the rule had the effect of pushing a certain group of students off the teams and out the door. Solving problems in a system without simply transferring a problem from one part of the system to another is a delicate business.

"Cause and effect are not closely related in time and space" (p. 63). In simple situations, seeing a direct and timely relationship between cause and effect is common. For example, children learn very quickly that if they don't share their toys and play nicely, they are likely to be removed from their play group. But direct cause-and-effect relationships like these are uncommon in complex systems such as our organizations. For example, in the "problem" example above, cause and effect were not what this well-intended group of educators expected them to be.

"Small changes can produce big results—but the areas of highest leverage are often the least obvious" (p. 63). In systems thinking, the most obvious solutions don't work. Setting a grade point average cutoff for participation is the most obvious solution for dealing with student athletes who are not doing well academically. The only problem is that it doesn't have the desired effect (pp. 57-67). A powerful example of a small change that led to a dynamic impact is that of Rosa Parks, in 1955, in Montgomery, Alabama. She refused to give up her seat for a white man and move to the back of the bus. Her act sparked the civil rights movement across the United States.

We know from chaos theory that often some small, insignificant action strategically placed can result in significant and lasting improvements. These are called *high-leverage* changes. The problem with such changes is that they are not obvious and not closely connected in time and space to the problem at hand.

Although difficult, it is possible to find high-leverage changes. Senge (1990) recommends that learning to see the underlying structures, patterns, and assumptions that drive thinking and action in organizations—instead of simply reacting to events—points us in the right direction.

▨ Reflection

Think of a problem you would like to solve. What is its root cause? To get at the root cause, ask yourself why you have the problem. Then ask why again and again in response to your answer. (Take as much time as you need to do this.) Then ask yourself and others what else might be contributing to this problem. This deeper inquiry will help you get at the underlying causes of the problem. Does your example also illustrate that cause and effect are not closely related in time and space?

Consider what solutions would address the underlying cause and then play out the implementation of these solutions. Who would be affected? How? What would be the costs and benefits across the system? Would implementation inadvertently harm people in other parts of the system?

▨ Notes

_____

_____

_____

_____

_____

_____

_____

▨ DAY 29: Identifying Organizational Character

*Character is the . . . personality of the . . . organization; it is the
DNA of the organizational life form. It is the organization's
character that makes it feel and act like itself.*

—William Bridges

Identifying and understanding the organization's character is central to leading any change effort. Knowing its character can help you better plan and
carry out the various stages of your change initiative.

An organization's character is analogous to the 16 personality types,
based on the work of Carl Jung (1921/1971), Isabel Briggs Myers et al.
(1998), and Katherine Cook Briggs. Just as knowing your own personality
type can help you better manage yourself and lead others more effectively, organizations that know their own characters can also manage themselves more
effectively.

An organization's character comes from four major sources:

1. *The character of the profession.* All lines of business, industries, and
   professions have their own characters. For example, education is very
   different from the military or the ministry.

2. *The influence of business itself.* When organizations, including
   schools, try to operate in a more businesslike manner, the orientation
   itself affects the organization's character.

3. *The personality types of the employees.* Research shows that certain
   types of personalities are attracted to certain occupations and lines of
   work. An organization with a model type of "Introverted Intuitors"
   will be very different from an organization with a majority of "Extraverted Sensors." (See Book One, Days 3, 6, 9, and 11.)

4. *The personality types of the leaders of the organization.* Leaders, especially strong ones, leave their marks on organizations.

▨ Reflection

Here is a sample. Think about the following questions. If you need help
remembering what each dichotomy means, go back to Book One:

- Is your organization introverted or extraverted? When considering a
  change effort, extraverted organizations look to their external environment for direction, whereas those who are introverted look internally.

- Is your organization sensing or intuitive? Sensing organizations tend
  to implement change incrementally, whereas intuitive organizations
  lean more toward transformational change.

- Is your organization thinking or feeling? Thinking organizations put more emphasis on completion of the change tasks, whereas feeling organizations emphasize the impact of the change on people.

- Is your organization judging or perceiving? Judging organizations drive toward decision making and closure in a change effort, whereas perceiving organizations are more inclined to keep their options open and seek more information.

Can you guess your organization's character? Is it INFP, ESTJ, or INTP? (See Book One, Day 14 for definitions.) And what does its character reveal about how it handles change? What can you do to build in an awareness of organizational character on your leadership team and into your implementation plan?

▧ Notes

_____

_____

_____

_____

_____

_____

_____

_____

▧ DAY 30: Examining Change History

Those who do not remember the past are condemned to repeat it.

—George Santayana

One factor often overlooked in systemic reform efforts is an organization's change history. *Change history* refers to how the organization has handled changes in the past.

Change history is important for two reasons. First, staff members have recollections of how the organization responded in the past. If change efforts have been successful, the staff will expect new attempts to enjoy success. If the track record shows many failed attempts, then the mind-set of the staff will be that the next change will similarly be doomed to failure.

Second, the staff's expectations are likely to be accurate and on target. Success breeds success; past failure suggests future failure unless people believe that something will be different on this occasion.

How do you know what to look for in your organization's change history? Here is a list of questions to ask yourself:

- Did leaders support prior change efforts?

- Were prior change efforts well communicated?

- Did leaders anticipate and plan for the impact of the changes on staff?

- Did the leaders adequately address the needs of individuals?

- Did the leaders commit the resources necessary to fully implement the change?

- Did the leaders model the behaviors they wanted to see in others as the result of the change?

A typical organization pattern is to initiate major change but fail to provide support for its full implementation. As a result, a change remains only partially implemented, dies out after two or three years, or is displayed by some other change.

If this has been the pattern in your organization, then staff and stakeholders are likely to be skeptical of the latest effort. Leaders have to overcome the effects of prior failures and the lingering institutional history to ensure current success. There may be skeptics who won't commit until they see whether this attempt is going to be different. As a leader, you must negotiate for the resources you need in order to implement the changes for which you are responsible.

▨ Reflection

What do you know about your organization's change history? If you don't know about it, how can you find out?

If you know the change history, what does it suggest you need to do to make your current reform initiative successful?

▨ Notes

_____

_____

_____

_____

_____

_____

_____

_____

_____

_____

▨ DAY 31: Launching and Sustaining Change Initiatives

Today's successful . . . leaders will be those who are most flexible of mind. An ability to embrace new ideas, routinely challenge old ones, and live with paradox will be the effective leader's premier trait. Further, the challenge is for a lifetime.

—Tom Peters

How do you know if your organization is ready to embark on a major change initiative and be successful? Organizations that are prepared to do so have characteristics different from those that are not. Many of the characteristics required for implementing change have been discussed in the contemplations in Book Two. These, along with a few others, are summarized in the checklist below.

Leaders of organizations that are prepared to launch and sustain major change initiatives do the following:

1. Involve the appropriate stakeholders

2. Think systemically

3. Have a compelling vision that is shared throughout the organization

4. Cultivate a high level of urgency for change

5. Think and act in terms of "both/and" rather than "either/or"

6. Challenge assumptions and mental models

7. Use data for decision making

8. Regularly take time for reflection

9. Empower people at all levels

10. Create structures with minimal hierarchy, fewer layers, and just the essential rules

11. Regularly conduct environmental scans to determine any changes in external influences on the organization and/or customer surveys

12. Exhibit a high level of risk taking, courage, and avoidance of blame

13. Identify what remains the same and what changes

14. Manage the key elements of change

15. Value continuous improvement

16. Commit the appropriate level of resources to support the change, including as much professional development as necessary

17. Promote resiliency in people and the organization

18. Designate benchmarks and acknowledge achievement of the benchmarks

Organizations today don't have the luxury of being able to reject or accept the opportunity to change. They must change, or they will cease to exist. The only open question is how successful they will be with whatever change initiatives they undertake.

▨ Reflection

How does your organization rate on this checklist? Some single items (Numbers 1, 4, 7, and 15, for example) can instantaneously kill a change initiative if they are not attended to properly.

If your organization isn't ready to take on a major change effort but needs to, what can you do to increase its readiness?

▨ Notes

Bibliography

Anderson, B. (1993). The stages of systemic change. *Educational Leadership,* *51*(1), 14-17.

Barrett, R. (1999). The power of purpose. *The Inner Edge,* 2(4), 20-22.

Bershad, C., & Mundry, S. (2000). Playing to learn: Systems change game challenges and teaches. *ENC Focus,* 7(1), 24-27.

Block, P. (1991). *The empowered manager: Positive political skills at work.* San Francisco: Jossey-Bass.

Conner, D. R. (1992). *Managing at the speed of change.* New York: Villard Books.

Conner, D. R. (1993). *Managing at the speed of change: How resilient managers succeed and prosper where others fail.* New York: Villard Books.

Conner, D. R. (1998). *Leading at the edge of chaos.* New York: John Wiley.

Covey, S. R. (1992). *Principle-based leadership.* London: Simon & Schuster.

Covey, S. R. (1996). Three roles of the leader in the new paradigm. In I. F. Hesselbein, M. Goldsmith, and B. Beckhard (Eds.), *The leader of the future.* San Francisco: Jossey-Bass.

Fritz, R. (1989). *The path of least resistance.* New York: Fawcett-Columbine.

Fullan, M. (1993). *Change forces: Probing the depths of educational reform.* London: Falmer.

Garmston, R. J., & Wellman, B. M. (1999). *The adaptive school: A sourcebook for developing collaborative groups.* Norwood, MA: Christopher-Gordon.

Hall, G., & Hord, S. (2001). *Implementing change: Patterns, principles, and potholes.* Needham Heights, MA: Allyn & Bacon.

Holzman, M. (1993). What is systemic change? *Educational Leadership, 51*(1), 18.

Isaacson, N., & Bamberg, J. (1992). Can schools become learning organizations? *Educational Leadership, 50*(3), 42-44.

Jung, C. J. (1971). *Psychological types.* Princeton, NJ: Princeton University Press. (Original work published 1921)

Kaser, J. S., & Horsley, D. (1998a). *Description of a change inventory process.* Albuquerque, NM: Kaser and Associates.

Kaser, J. S., & Horsley, D. (1998b). *Sources of resistance.* Albuquerque, NM: Kaser and Associates.

Kotter, J. P. (1996). *Leading change.* Boston: Harvard Business School Press.

Kübler-Ross, E. (1970). *On death and dying.* New York: Macmillan.

Loucks-Horsley, S., & Stiegelbauer, S. (1991). Using knowledge of change to guide staff development. In A. Lieberman and L. Miller (Eds.), *Staff development for education in the '90s: New demands, new realities, new perspectives.* New York: Teachers College Press.

Myers, I. B., McCaulley, M. H., Quenk, N. L., & Hammer, A. L. (1998). *MBTI manual.* Palo Alto, CA: Consulting Psychologists Press.

Senge, P. M. (1990). *The fifth discipline.* New York: Doubleday.

Senge, P. M., Kleiner, A., Roberts, C., Ross, R. B., Roth, G., & Smith, B. J. (1999). *The dance of change.* New York: Doubleday.

Senge, P. M., Roberts, C., Ross, R. B., Smith, B. J., & Kleiner, A. (1994). *The fifth discipline fieldbook.* New York: Doubleday.

Vaill, P. B. (1992). *Managing as a performing art.* New York: Villard Books.

Book Three

▧ Leading Learning

Book Three is a collection of thoughts and inspirations on lifelong learning. The leader's role is to carefully design and nurture the conditions that promote learning for all—individuals, teams, and organizations. These contemplations provide basic information to help leaders promote lifelong learning for themselves and those with whom they work.

The contemplations in this book explore a number of key issues related to lifelong learning and especially, professional development as one approach to meeting lifelong learning needs. For example, why has lifelong learning become so important in our society? How has the need for lifelong learning affected organizations that provide professional development for their people? How does the "new" professional development in education differ from the "old"? How does one develop a commitment to lifelong learning, and why is that important? What constitutes a professional development activity?

Other questions include the following: What are the key factors in the design and conduct of many different types of professional development? How does one design professional development that reflects how people learn best? How does one go about providing professional development for individuals, teams, and organizations? How does one evaluate professional development? And finally, how can one be an effective leader of learning?

The first contemplation focuses on a framework for planning professional development programs for individuals, teams, or organizations. Its principles underlie all the other contemplations in this section. The contemplations that follow discuss the changing nature of learning, approaches to quality professional development, key issues in the design and implementation of a variety of learning experiences, team learning, evaluating professional development, and being an effective leader of learning.

PART I

A Framework for Planning

What do a two-day retreat to learn teamwork skills, a mentoring program for new staff, and an online course on classroom management for beginning teachers have in common?

They all are professional development programs of one type or another. And to produce the greatest impact, each must be designed to address its particular needs and incorporate the components of effective professional development.

Designing professional development experiences according to a framework is one way of ensuring that all the components have been accounted for and/or are in place. The framework presented in Day 1 serves as such a guide.

▨ DAY 1: Designing Professional Development

*A bridge, like professional development, is a critical link
between where one is and where one wants to be. A bridge that
works in one place almost never works in another. Each bridge
requires careful design that considers its purpose, who will use it,
the conditions that exist at its anchor points . . . and the resources
required to construct it. Similarly, each professional development
program . . . requires a careful and unique design.*

—Susan Loucks-Horsley

Although there is still more for research to uncover about the nature of learning, there is a solid base of information about the characteristics of effective learning experiences for adults.

As the above quotation points out, each learning experience is in many ways unique. There is no one right way to approach the learning. There are, however, frameworks for designing learning experiences based on what we know to be effective.

Leaders of learning are often in the position of designing, or suggesting that others design, professional development activities for individuals or groups. Effective professional development addresses a number of important and fairly specific issues or factors. It isn't thrown together; it isn't cookie cutter; it isn't the innovation du jour. It is consciously and deliberately designed.

Here is one framework for designing professional development for both individual and group learning (Loucks-Horsley, Hewson, Love, & Stiles, 1998). This framework underlies all subsequent contemplations in this book on leading learning. That is why it is the topic of Day 1.

For a learning program to be effective, it needs to have the following:

- A set of goals for the learning and a set of expected outcomes

- A plan for proceeding over time

- A set of actions that implement the plan

- Reflection on and evaluation of each major component of the design and revisions made to the plan, outcomes, and goals, as appropriate

Designers of learning opportunities must consider four important types of planning input (see Figure 3.1):

1. *Knowledge and beliefs.* The design must reflect the knowledge base on learning, teaching, the nature of the subject matter, professional development, the change process, and the fundamental beliefs that will guide you (e.g., that all people can learn).

Figure 3.1. Professional Development Design Framework

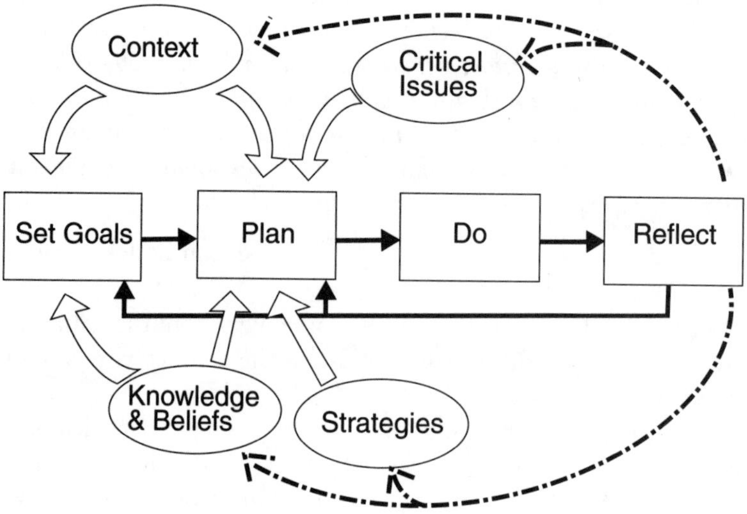

SOURCE: Loucks-Horsley, Hewson, Love, and Stiles (1998, p. 17).

2. *Context.* The design must suit the context in which the learning will take place and the teaching will occur. The context includes learners, teachers, practices, policies, resources, organizational culture, organizational structure, history of professional development, and other stakeholders, such as parents and community members.

3. *Critical issues.* The design must take into account those elements that will affect—either positively or negatively—the success of the learning. Examples include equity and diversity, professional culture, leadership, capacity building for sustainability, scaling up, public support, effective use of standards, time for professional development, and evaluation and assessment.

4. *Strategies.* The design must reflect the different approaches to learning that are most appropriate for the learner given the context for learning.

These factors and the planning model combine to create a dynamic whole that must be considered as you design learning experiences for adults in your organization. The factors all influence and contribute to each other and continuously change, so one must stay tuned to the environment to adapt to these changing circumstances.

▨ Reflection

Think about some professional development program that you have been a part of and answer the following questions:

- What were its goals and outcomes? How do you know?

- Was a plan implemented?

- Were there evaluation and reflection components on the process and results?

- What assumptions did the learning program make about the nature of teaching, learning, the content, and the change process? How were they guided by research?

- Did the learning program take the context of the organization into account? If so, how?

- What strategies of teaching and learning did the program employ? Were they the right ones for the situation? Would you have chosen different strategies? If so, describe what and why.

- How successful was the learning program? How do you know? Were there any critical issues that the program did or didn't address that affected the outcome?

If you had been in charge of this professional development program, what would you have done differently?

▨ Notes

PART II

Emerging Practices

Ideas about how people learn have undergone considerable change in the past two decades. Learning is now seen as a lifelong activity rather than something that is completed in formal schooling early in our lives. Individuals who function as effective adults—in the workplace and in other aspects of their lives—are committed to lifelong learning. Organizations, too, must be committed to having a workforce that has the knowledge and skills necessary for functioning in the "Information Age." In education, knowledge about teaching and learning is increasing at an exponential rate. It is no longer sufficient to merely deliver information about new skills and knowledge; professional developers must help educators make sense of and use new skills and knowledge effectively. There are several ways of looking at past professional development practices and comparing them to emerging practices.

The following seven contemplations (Days 2–8) explore these ideas.

▧ DAY 2: Contemporary Professional Development

The new professional development must be different and much more powerful, and it will involve solving problems and collaborating at levels that we have never even contemplated.

—Anthony Alvarado

What did professional development in education used to look like? What is it starting to look like now?

In the field of education, most professional learning was provided through in-service workshops. Rarely did teachers have a voice in the types of sessions they attended or the opportunity to connect their new learning with their own practice. Too often, professional development touched only the surface of some content with short overviews and no follow-up.

Today, professional development is moving in a different direction. In-service has expanded to include not only training programs but also many ongoing and job-embedded approaches to professional development. Here are some of the distinguishing characteristics of this new approach:

- It is directly related to the school's goals and the staff's needs in meeting these goals.

- It supports teachers in making explicit connections between what they do and what their students learn.

- It is designed to build a learning community in which all take responsibility for learning over time and the staff work collegially to share knowledge, insight, and experience.

- It empowers the staff to design, conduct, and follow through on their own learning.

- It takes learning to deeper levels; learning is more in depth.

- It provides follow-up support and time for practice and reflection.

- It establishes a safe environment in which the staff can take risks without fear of failure or ridicule.

- It holds the staff accountable for their learning and its impact on outcomes.

- It continuously monitors and evaluates the successes, difficulties, and failures of the new approach.

One elementary school has adopted an interesting approach to its professional development. Whenever any staff member (including the principal) is gone for professional development, he or she posts a sign on the door that says, *Out Learning.* Upon returning, each staff member is responsible for writing a report on the experience for others. Students and colleagues are encouraged to ask what the professional development participant learned from his or her experience.

▨ Reflection

If you have been with your organization for some time, write a list of about a dozen words that describe the professional development as practiced 8 to 10 years ago. Now, jot down a dozen words that describe your recent professional development. What differences do you see? What accounts for these differences? If you don't see changes, why not? Is your professional development stuck, or is it evolving? If it is stuck, what can you do to get it out of the mire?

▨ Notes

_____

_____

_____

_____

_____

_____

_____

▨ DAY 3: Lifelong Learning

The future ain't what it used to be.

—Yogi Berra

The changes in professional development are not occurring in a vacuum. They are the direct result of changes going on in our society—the movement toward learning as a lifelong activity.

Life used to be simpler. You learned what you needed to know at home, in school, or on the job. And once you learned it, it served you well for the rest of your life.

Perhaps you bought a new computer program and taught yourself how to use it. Or if you were a teacher, the adoption of a new textbook led you to teach somewhat differently. Maybe a new appliance or piece of equipment changed the way you worked at home or work. But for the most part, you knew what you needed to know for life. There were simply fewer developments and breakthroughs in most fields over lengthy periods of time.

The advent of the Information Age has turned learning upside down. Now, what you acquire from your family, in formal education (kindergarten through graduate school), or on your job is just the beginning. The short shelf life of knowledge has transformed how people think about learning. New developments and breakthroughs occur at an exponential rate.

The term *lifelong learning* more accurately describes the challenge that people now face. Progressing through your career, you need to sharpen and expand your knowledge and skills to continue to be successful. Otherwise, you, like knowledge, become outdated. Just think of what you have had to learn since you ended your formal schooling.

The constant press for ongoing learning is creating the need for new environments and new attitudes toward learning. Leaders need to create the motivation and commitment to learn among people in their organizations and create the environments—time, structures, and incentives—for learning to happen.

Acquiring new knowledge and skills is often exciting. On occasion, it can be a major challenge, especially if, for a time, you are rendered incompetent, feel uncomfortable, feel out of control, or lack confidence. These are all normal human responses to learning something new, especially at the beginning. Fortunately, they diminish as you build proficiency.

▨ Reflection

Think for a moment about your work environment. What developments in society contribute to you and your colleagues needing to enhance your knowledge and skills? To what extent do your colleagues see learning as a lifelong activity? Which ones seem reluctant to acquire new knowledge and skills? How do you know?

As a leader, what can you do to help your colleagues become continuous learners? Do you model that behavior yourself? If so, in what way? If not, how can you change your attitudes and practices?

▨ Notes

_____

_____

_____

_____

_____

_____

_____

_____

_____

_____

_____

▨ DAY 4: Personal Mastery

*Learning does not occur in any enduring fashion unless
it is sparked by people's own ardent interest and curiosity.*

—From *The Fifth Discipline Fieldbook*, Peter Senge et al.

What is personal mastery? How is it a different approach to learning? How can it help you become a better leader while encouraging leadership in others?

Peter Senge (1990) uses the term *personal mastery* to describe a quality of people who display vision and dedication. If you have personal mastery, you are committed to lifelong acquisition of new knowledge and skills and to improving and expanding your existing skills. For example, a master craftsman who continuously perfects his craft and an athlete who keeps improving her performance demonstrate personal mastery. Personal mastery provides the clarity and ability to produce for ourselves the results we want.

Senge (1990) identifies three characteristics of personal mastery: a strong sense of personal vision, a commitment to continually learning to see reality more clearly, and continually clarifying what is most important to us.

Leaders have a twofold responsibility of incorporating these three characteristics into their lives and creating environments in which others in their organizations can do the same.

Having a personal vision means you are clear and passionate about what you want. A commitment to keeping reality in sharp focus is a commitment to being honest with yourself—usually by grounding your beliefs in facts and research-based data. Clarifying what is most important helps you focus on the important aspects of your life and avoid getting waylaid by that which is less significant.

See Book Two, Day 27, for additional information on personal mastery.

▨ Reflection

Describe your own commitment to personal mastery. In what aspects of your life have you demonstrated personal mastery? How has this changed over the years?

As a leader, what do you do to help others develop their own sense of personal mastery? Have you ever discussed your vision with your coworkers or questioned how your collective work supports your personal visions? To what extent do you value speaking the truth about your reality and encouraging others to do the same? How often do you discuss with your coworkers what is most important? As you go through each day, do you ask whether your actions contribute significantly to what you are committed to attaining?

▨ Notes

▨ DAY 5: Learning Organizations

*Workforce training and constant retraining . . . must climb to
the top of the agenda of the individual firm and the nation.*

—Tom Peters

Organizations cannot renew themselves without renewing their people. With
the short shelf life of knowledge, ongoing development of staff is essential for
organizations to succeed. It is one component of being what Peter Senge
(1990) calls a *learning organization:* "An organization that is continually expanding its capacity to create its future" (p. 14).

As Senge (1990) says,

> Different people in the same structure tend to produce qualitatively
> similar results. When there are problems, or performance fails to live
> up to what is intended, it is easy to find someone or something to
> blame. But, more often than we realize, systems cause their own cri-
> ses, not external forces or individuals' mistakes. (p. 40)

Organizational problems require organizational solutions, and one of these is
continuous learning.

Leaders are challenged to build organizations that learn. One way they do
this is to promote a continuous cycle of planning, doing, and reflecting. Another way includes matching professional development to real performance
needs. These needs are identified through data on (a) customer satisfaction
with services and products and (b) employees' perceptions of their own needs.
Then, both sets of needs are screened through the lens of the organization's
vision. An organization can also set up collegial work groups for sharing experience and knowledge. Regardless of the approach, these activities never end.
After a cycle is completed, the process starts all over again.

▨ Reflection

Think about an organization you have been involved with that did not
have a commitment to lifelong learning. What happened to this organization?
What did people do if they wanted to strengthen their knowledge or skills?
Did they have to provide all or part of the resources themselves? How long
did they stay with the organization?

Now, recall the opposite situation—a situation where you were encouraged to learn continuously. How did the organization manifest its commitment? How did you and your colleagues feel? What difference did this make
in the organization?

What about the organization you are part of now? What can you do to
promote a culture of continuous learning?

▧ Notes

_____

_____

_____

_____

_____

_____

_____

_____

_____

_____

_____

_____

▧ DAY 6: Additive and Transformative Learning

There is little evidence for and a strong argument against
the proposition that professional development as traditionally
organized and conducted is effective in helping teachers
understand the core of the reforms.

—Charles Thompson and John Zeuli

What is new in professional development?

In Book One, Day 25 explores the difference between transactional and transformational leadership. Simply put, in transactional leadership, the traditional approach is for leaders to lead and followers to follow. Transformational leadership is very different. With more complex dynamics, leadership is shared.

There is a parallel in professional development, although the terms are slightly different: *additive and transformative learning.* In additive learning, the goal is to acquire new skills and incorporate them into an existing repertoire. The goal of transformative learning is to change deeply held beliefs, knowledge, and habits of practice. Additive learning alone will not suffice when new ways of thinking about something are also needed (Thompson & Zeuli, 1999).

The transformative approach to professional development is new and cutting edge. Transformation focuses on designing learning experiences that challenge participants' current thinking and often startle them into new beliefs. The old way can be described as *evolutionary tinkering* within the traditional paradigm. This contrasts sharply with revolutionary changes that transform the basic thinking and beliefs of participants.

In education, transformational learning occurs when teachers engage with student thinking and assess how well their current methods address the students' learning. Teachers are likely to discover that using the same old approaches to teach more challenging content just is not effective. They see the need to rethink what they do and how they interact with students. These experiences produce discomfort with current practice and the need to adapt to create better outcomes.

Both additive and transformative professional development may be necessary. Additive learning is appropriate for developing new skills. However, learners must understand the assumptions and beliefs that guide the skill; or they may learn the skill well but lack the understanding of why they are using it. Transformative learning focuses more on making shifts in assumptions and beliefs and helping learners understand why a new approach might be necessary. The emphasis of education today is moving toward integrating both transformative and additive learning.

▨ Reflection

Think about the professional development that has transpired in your organization. Would you describe it as more additive or transformative, or as both? Give some examples to support your answer.

What type of professional development seems appropriate in your setting? If you think that your organization needs professional development that is more transformative, what can you as a leader do to help make that happen? If you think both additative and trasformative learning are needed, how might you integrate them?

▨ Notes

▨ DAY 7: Reflection and Cognitive Apprenticeships

Effective professional development programs of the future will break from the traditional mold because the new century requires new forms.
—From *Teaching and Teaching Development*, Ann Lieberman et al.

Just how differently is transformative professional development implemented? Here are five distinguishing characteristics (Thompson & Zeuli, 1999):

1. It creates cognitive dissonance, a disruption in someone's thinking, causing them to struggle to make sense of something that doesn't fit with their current ideas.

2. It provides time, contexts, and support for teachers to resolve this dissonance by engaging over time with facilitators who have had experience in coaching and mentoring.

3. It ensures that the dissonance-creating and dissonance-resolving activities are relevant to the participant.

4. It provides a means for participants to develop new practices that are congruent with the new ideas they are constructing.

5. It ensures participants of continuing help in the cycle of surfacing the new issues and problems they will encounter, gaining new understandings from these experiences, translating these new understandings from them, and recycling through the above process.

Two models of learning underlie these requirements: reflective problem solving and cognitive apprenticeship. *Reflective problem solving* entails individual or collaborative efforts to resolve some puzzle or conflict. An example of this is when a decision point or dilemma emerges and existing ideas are challenged by new information arising from observed or actual practice.

Cognitive apprenticeship refers to an approach to learning that results from connecting a novice with an expert. The more experienced person (a) models the desired performance and provides support for the novice to try out new behaviors or (b) gives feedback on the novice's performance and how it might be improved. Eventually, the expert gradually withdraws support as the novice is able to function independently.

▨ Reflection

Think of a learning experience that created cognitive dissonance for you. What were you thinking and feeling? How did you resolve it? We often resolve dissonance by rejecting the new idea and holding fast to our prior beliefs. Without challenge and support to get to the other side of dissonance, learning will not occur.

Now, recall a typical professional development event in your organization for which you have had some responsibility. How is it similar to or different from the description above? If it is very different, what factors need to be in place to move toward transformative staff development? What can you do to help bring about this shift? In what places do you need to have a balance between transformative and additive learning?

▨ Notes

▧ DAY 8: Aligning Assumptions and Behaviors

If teachers are to teach for deeper understanding through processes that are more engaging of their students, the [professional development] must mirror the type of instruction that schools would like to see practiced in the classrooms.

—Dennis Sparks

Alignment is one of the key words in reform. For example, we talk about curriculum and professional development being aligned with local and state standards. Likewise, we encourage organizations to align structures with their visions and missions.

Another area of alignment is ensuring the congruency between what we believe and how we behave. An example is identifying our underlying assumptions about teaching and learning and determining whether our behavior is consistent with our beliefs. When you examine what is going on with professional development in education today, several inconsistencies stand out (see Table 3.1).

Table 3.1 Examples of Misalignment

What We Say	*What We Do*
That teacher learning is the centerpiece of effective change	Provide a few hours of in-service each year
That students should be independent, self-directed learners	Give teachers little say regarding the content or process of their own staff development
That teaching is a complex process of decision making requiring a wide range of instructional strategies to meet individual learner needs	Limit professional development to workshops
That every child, every teacher, and every organization is in some ways unique, and programs need to be tailored to meet individual needs	Reduce professional development to "one size fits all"
That change is long-term	Direct professional development resources to "one-shot" workshops without follow-up support
That change is systemwide	Work with volunteers, the early adopters, which produces pockets of change rather than systemwide change

These inconsistencies may have several different causes:

- We have not examined our underlying assumptions and do not recognize the discrepancies in our behavior.
- We do not see the lack of alignment as a problem that needs to be addressed.
- Changes in organizational culture normally lag behind other types of institutional changes. Adopting a new curriculum is much easier than getting everyone to become proficient in teaching it.
- Existing resources are insufficient to support the change effort.

▨ Reflection

Which of these incongruities exist in your organization's professional development programs? What other incongruities not listed in the table can you identify?

What are the causes for these discrepancies? How can you engage your colleagues in looking for and surfacing misalignments and inconsistencies?

For each "What we say" item, write a "What we do" statement. For example, if you believe that teacher learning is the centerpiece of effective change, then your professional development program would be substantial (in terms of time) and ongoing.

▨ Notes

PART III
Context and Strategies

Two key components of the framework for designing professional development (Day 1) are context and strategies. Each is explored in detail in this section. In addition, the specifications of three alternative approaches to professional development are presented: coaching/mentoring, professional networks, and action research.

▨ DAY 9: Contextual Professional Development

*We are learning that professional development that increases
teacher knowledge is more likely to occur when such development
. . . respects local knowledge (i.e., problems and practices that
attend to the particulars of a context).*

—Ann Lieberman and Lynne Miller

When it comes to professional development programs, "off the shelf" and
"one size fits all" simply do not work. And there is a reason why these programs don't work. It is called *context.*

Skilled professional developers know to take context into account if their
professional development programs are to be successful. Here are the major
factors that constitute context (Loucks-Horsley et al., 1998, pp. 173-190):

- Differences among the participants who are going through the professional development, such as prior knowledge of the content and learning style

- How participants intend to use the knowledge and skills they are
acquiring

- Policies and practices of the organization in which the participants are
working

- Structure of the organization

- Amount of resources supporting the professional development

- History of professional development in the organization

- Role of stakeholders in the professional development

- Internal and external political issues

- Competing demands for resources, including time

So, it is easy to see why a "very good" professional development program may not work in an environment in which, for example, participants
are very knowledgeable of the content or lack the resources to support the
full program. That is why "good" always has to be followed with "good for
what purpose?"

▨ Reflection

Think of a professional development program in your organization that
worked well and one that didn't. What role did context play in the success or
failure of the programs?

Think of a program that is in the planning stage. To what extent is context being taken into account? What can you as a leader do to ensure that contextual issues are being addressed?

▨ Notes

▨ DAY 10: Strategies for Professional Networks

*Every . . . professional development plan uses a variety of
strategies in combination with another to form a unique design.
Each strategy is one piece of the puzzle.*

—From *Designing Professional Development
for Science and Mathematics Teachers*,
Susan Loucks-Horsley, et al.

When you think of adult learning, what specific strategies come to mind? Do you think of formal settings for lectures and/or media presentations, with or without a few experiential activities interspersed?

Traditionally, organizations have viewed professional development for adults in terms of sending employees to workshops, institutes, courses, or seminars or hosting these events on-site.

We now think of professional development in much broader terms. It can include coaching and mentoring, study groups, professional networks, partnerships, technology, or action research. In fact, some of these approaches to professional development may actually be much more effective than traditional workshops, institutes, courses, and seminars.

Here is a list of 15 strategies for professional development of educators of science and mathematics that offer a broader view of the strategies available for professional development (Loucks-Horsley et al., 1998, pp. 43-44):

Immersion

1. Immersion in inquiry into science or mathematics—engaging in the kinds of learning that teachers are expected to practice with their students

2. Immersion in the world of scientists and mathematicians—participating in an intensive experience in a work setting in which the subject matter is used, such as working with a scientist on a research project

Curriculum

3. Curriculum implementation—learning, using, and refining one's use of a particular set of instructional materials

4. Curriculum replacement units—implementing a unit of instruction (curriculum replacement units) that addresses one topic in a way that illustrates effective teaching techniques

5. Curriculum development and adaptation—creating new instructional materials and strategies or tailoring existing ones

Examining practice

6. Action research—examining teachers' own teaching and their students' learning by engaging in a research project in the classroom

7. Case discussions—examining written narratives or videotapes of classroom events

8. Examining student work and student thinking and scoring assessments—carefully examining students' work and products to understand their thinking and to identify appropriate instructional strategies and materials

Collaborative work

9. Study groups—engaging in regular collaborative interactions around topics identified by the group

10. Coaching and mentoring—working one-on-one in a coaching or mentoring role to help another teacher improve teaching and learning

11. Partnerships with scientists and mathematicians in business, industry, and universities—working collaboratively with practicing scientists and mathematicians to improve teacher content knowledge, instructional materials, and access to facilities

12. Professional networks—setting up professional networks by linking in person or electronically with other teachers to explore common concerns

Vehicles and mechanisms

13. Workshops, institutes, courses, and seminars—using workshops, institutes, courses, and seminars to focus intensely on topics of interest and to learn from experts

14. Technology for professional development—using various kinds of technology to learn content and pedagogy (e.g., online courses or distance learning)

15. Developing professional developers—developing staff to be professional developers through building the skills and understanding of content and pedagogy necessary to create learning experiences for others

▨ Reflection

Consider the professional development going on in your organization. Does it implement any of the strategies listed above? Which ones?

If your organization has a more narrow definition of professional development, could any of the alternative strategies better help you achieve your goals? Which ones would work in your setting? What would you like to try and why? As a leader, what can you do to broaden the concept of what constitutes professional development?

▨ Notes

_____

_____

_____

_____

_____

_____

_____

_____

▨ DAY 11: Situational Strategies

The professional development designer's challenge is to assemble a combination of learning activities that best meets the special goals and context.

—From *Designing Professional Development for Teachers of Science and Mathematics*, Susan Loucks-Horsley, et al.

Given a specific context and all these different strategies for professional development, how does one know which approach to choose?

Think back to the framework for planning professional development. First, consider your goals; what outcomes do you expect? Next, look at the context, knowledge and beliefs, and critical issues involved. Then, go to the different professional development strategies and ask yourself the question, "Given this context and our goals, which strategies are most appropriate?" You can answer that question by looking at the characteristics of each strategy (see Loucks-Horsley et al., 1998). These include the underlying assumptions, key elements, and implementation requirements.

As an example, let's look at one approach you are probably familiar with, coaching and mentoring. Here are the specifications—underlying assumptions, key elements, and implementation requirements (Loucks-Horsley et al., 1998, pp. 125-132):

Underlying assumptions

There are three underlying assumptions to coaching and mentoring:
- An individual's reflection on his or her own practice can be enhanced by another's observations and perceptions.
- Those working to master new procedures, processes, or materials can benefit from ongoing assistance.
- There are professionals whose experience, expertise, and observations are valuable sources of knowledge, skill development, and inspiration for their peers or for novices.

Key elements

For coaching and mentoring to be successful, the following conditions must be in place:
- A focus on learning or improvement
- Opportunities for interaction, including feedback

Implementation requirements
- A climate of trust and collegiality
- A long-term commitment to the relationship
- Skill building in coaching and mentoring
- Administrative support for the relationship

If all these factors are in place, one can reasonably expect a significant change in knowledge, attitudes, and/or skills on the part of the person being coached or mentored. For profiles of other approaches to staff development, see *Designing Professional Development for Teachers of Science and Mathematics* (Loucks-Horsley et al., 1998).

▨ Reflection

Knowing what you do now about coaching and mentoring, come up with a professional development context in which this strategy would be appropriate and effective. Why do you think it would work?

Next, come up with a situation in which this strategy would not be appropriate or effective. Why wouldn't it work? What might work in its place?

Why do some strategies work in certain situations and not in others?

How can you help your colleagues look at professional development with the broader view of implementing multiple strategies rather than just offering courses, workshops, seminars, and institutes?

▨ Notes

_____

_____

_____

_____

_____

▨ DAY 12: Professional Networks

Rather than a linear, deficit approach, staff development is expanding to include networks, coalitions, and partnerships that provide a new model of teacher involvement and learning— one that not only encourages teacher knowledge, but also is far more sensitive to the contexts that help shape teacher practice.

—Ann Lieberman and Lynne Miller

Professional networks are among the newest professional development strategies made possible by electronic communication. According to Loucks-Horsley et al. (1998), networks are organized professional communities that have a common theme or purpose. People join networks to share their knowledge and experience and to learn from each other.

Networks can exist within an organization; across several organizations; within a geographical region, including statewide and nationally; or within a professional association or field. Networks generally have specific goals and purposes, recruit members, and schedule activities. Common activities include regular meetings, seminars or institutes, and special interest groups. Electronic activities include listserves, newsletters or bulletin boards, and chat rooms.

One of the challenges of a network is keeping people connected and engaged. Effective networks have a system for updating members if they miss some event. Perhaps a "buddy" e-mails an update, or minutes are posted on the bulletin board. Networks can be formal (as described here) or much more informal. With the latter, a group of individuals forms to exchange information and get professional support. Activities are more likely to be scheduled on an "as needed" basis.

Professional networks have the following underlying assumptions (Loucks-Horsley et al., 1998, pp. 141-150):

- Adults are social by nature and benefit from interacting with others who have similar interests and concerns.

- Professionals have knowledge and experience to share, and such sharing can result in improvements in practice.

- Meaningful improvement in an area occurs best when members of a professional community share common beliefs and work together to achieve common goals.

Here are the key elements of a professional network:

- Members interact with each other.

- Membership is voluntary in most instances, and all interested persons are welcomed.

- Communication is effective and takes place in a number of different ways.
- The network promotes broad perspectives.
- A capable person manages the network.

Successful networks require the following:

- A clear focus of activity
- Size and logistical requirements (e.g., presence of a trained monitor to guide discussion)
- Mechanisms for communication
- Structures for monitoring progress and impact

Professional networks can provide a highly successful professional development strategy for individuals, especially those who are isolated or lack time to meet face-to-face. Individuals can develop a collegial community to explore some aspect of their field. The network also provides support, motivation, and stimulation and offers a venue to affirm professionals who are involved in major reforms in their organizations. There are a number of potential logistical problems with operating a network, such as stability, ownership, and pace of growth, which require constant monitoring. Leaders involved in organizing networks need to plan for these potential problems.

▨ Reflection

Here is a second application exercise, similar to the one for Day 10. Consider the professional development needs of the people in your organization, the framework for planning professional development, and the specifications of a professional network. Under what circumstances would establishing such a network be appropriate? When would it not be productive? How do you know? What are possible activities for your network?

▨ Notes

_____

_____

_____

◫ DAY 13: Action Research

That action research may not conform to conventional criteria of research rigor is much less important than that it takes a more democratic, empowering, and humanizing approach; assists locals in extending their own understanding of their situations; and helps them to resolve the problems they see as important.

—Egon G. Guba

A form of professional development that is gaining popularity is action research. Introduced by Kurt Lewin (1946), action research has been used in a number of settings, especially education. In *action research*, professionals examine their own work through data gathering, descriptive reporting, directed conversation, sharing among colleagues, and critical reflection. The goal is improved performance.

Action research is an excellent way of getting professionals involved in examining the outcomes of their own work, reflectively and thoughtfully. As a result, they usually have greater ownership in promoting changes indicated by their findings.

Action research as a professional development strategy includes the following (Loucks-Horsley et al., 1998, pp. 94-103):

Professionals
- They are intelligent, inquiring people who have important knowledge, skills, and experiences central to their fields.
- They experience professional growth by formulating their own questions and by gathering data to answer those questions.
- They are more likely to use effective practices when they are continuously investigating the results of their actions.

Key elements
- Using an action research cycle of planning, acting, observing, and reflecting
- Linking with sources of expertise from outside one's own organization
- Working collaboratively with others
- Documenting and sharing learning

Implementation requirements
- Access to research resources
- Time to carry out action research
- Administrative support
- Opportunities to share the results of the research

Benefits arise from both the process and product of action research. Professionals can acquire new knowledge and broaden their skills through action research. They generate new knowledge that can help their organizations make needed improvements, broaden the research base of their field, and reduce the gap between research and practice. All of these benefits are usually empowering experiences for the action researchers, contributing to their self-esteem, leadership activities, and status among colleagues.

Action research, however, is not for everybody. Novices in particular may need help gathering and analyzing data. Carrying out such research also takes a great deal of time and may not be seen as a legitimate activity by administrators (Loucks-Horsley et al., 1998). Leaders who organize action research projects must help participants enlist the support of administrators and other decision makers.

▨ Reflection

Have you used action research as a professional development strategy? If so, what needs did it meet? How did you introduce it to others? What were they able to accomplish? What was your role? What were the short-term, intermediate, and long-term results?

If you have never promoted action research as a professional development strategy, under what circumstances would you do so? How would you do so? What would your expected outcomes be? What would your role be in this endeavor? Who would you involve?

With a colleague or by yourself, brainstorm some questions you could try to investigate through action research.

▨ Notes

_____

_____

_____

_____

_____

PART IV
Designing Learning Experiences

There are numerous issues to take into account in designing learning experiences for people in your organization. How do they learn best? What have been their most powerful learning experiences in the past? How much of what they learn should focus on theory or philosophy and how much on the practical "What do I do tomorrow" questions? How can learning experiences be constructed so they are highly effective?

If the learning experience occurs in a group, how do the leaders make sure that their design is reflexive and that it is true to itself? In other words, does the learning experience allow the leaders to "walk their talk," to do what they suggest their participants do? Do they model the model? Do they teach about inquiry through inquiry?

Taking diversity into account is another key issue—both in the content of the learning experience and in the representation of participants themselves. Who has access to professional development opportunities in your setting? After developing a successful learning experience or professional development program, how does one involve others so the program's effects are more widespread?

Finally, how are learning experiences set up that incorporate results from research on how people learn best, including how they transfer their learning to their own practice?

The next nine contemplations (Days 14–22) address these questions.

▨ DAY 14: Examining Learning Styles

A critic once commented to Cézanne, "That doesn't look anything like a sunset." Pondering his painting, Cézanne responded, "Then you don't see sunsets the way I do."

—L. P. Martinez

Knowledge of how people learn best must drive professional development design. Think for a moment about how you learn best. How do you know how others learn best? What factors should you consider in answering these questions?

Gordon Lawrence (1993, p. 39) has identified four factors to consider when examining individuals' preferred learning styles:

- Cognitive style, our preferred or habitual patterns of mental functioning, including how we process information, how we form ideas, and how we make judgments

- Patterns of attitudes and interests that determine what we attend to in any learning situation

- An inclination to seek out learning environments which are compatible with our cognitive style, attitudes, and interests and to avoid those that are not

- An inclination to use certain learning tools and to avoid others

There are many ways to determine how you and others learn best. One way is through a *learning styles inventory;* various versions are available. Or you can simply ask yourself and others. Most adults have had sufficient life experience to know what works best for them.

In completing any kind of informal self-assessment, here are some questions to consider:

- What type of subject matter do you like and do best in?

- Which modality do you prefer (visual, auditory, or kinesthetic)?

- Do you prefer lectures, reading on your own, graphic displays, or hands-on activities?

- Would you rather learn by yourself or with other people?

- What are examples of the learning activities that have been the most exciting and valuable to you? What are their common characteristics?

- What is hardest for you to learn?

- What types of learning situations do you try to avoid?

Answers to these questions will give you and others greater insight into how you learn best. With the vast amount of knowledge and skills that people need during a lifetime, this information can be very useful in helping you determine the most effective and efficient way to learn for yourself and others.

▨ Reflection

Think about three or four of your colleagues who you think have different learning styles. At the same time, recall the different approaches to professional development discussed in Day 10. Which approaches do you think are most appropriate for which people? How do you know? If you are not sure, how would you find out?

Think about a recent learning situation in which you participated. To what extent did it fit your learning style? How much did you learn? How could the situation have been constructed differently to enhance your learning?

Now, recall a learning situation that you directed. It might have been a particular staff meeting or a more formal professional development event. In what ways did you take the learning preferences of different people into account? What do you think they learned? What could they have learned if the environment had been tailored more to their needs?

▨ Notes

_____

_____

_____

_____

_____

_____

▨ DAY 15: Powerful Learning Experiences

*Epiphany—any sudden and important manifestation
or realization.*

—Oxford English Dictionary

Whether we call it an "aha!" experience or the moment when "the light goes on," we have all had powerful learning experiences. These experiences often occur when we connect new information to something we already know and understand, and it takes us farther in our thinking.

An analysis of our "lightbulb" experiences can give us insight into how we learn best, what learning is most important to us, and the circumstances in which the learning occurs (Owen, Cox, & Watkins, 1994). Let's see whether this is the case for you.

▨ Reflection

Think about a learning experience in your life that had a powerful impact. It could have been an event from your formal schooling or any aspect of your life. It could be something that happened recently or a long time ago. You may recall it as being either pleasant or unpleasant.

First, recreate this experience in your mind. Imagine being in the situation again. What happened? What did you do? What were you feeling? What did others do? What was the impact? Did it occur then or later?

After you have a clear picture of the event, write a brief description of it.

Now, answer the following questions about your powerful learning experience:

- Where did your experience occur?

- What were the characteristics of the learning? Think in terms of the connections, the conditions, the environment, and resources available.

- Was there a teacher of some sort present? If so, what role did this person play? What role did you play in this experience?

- If your experience was positive, what would be necessary for it to be duplicated either within or outside of formal schooling?

- If your experience was negative, is this something that should be avoided? If so, what would be necessary to make sure that others did not have this same experience?

Only about 25 percent of people completing this exercise report that their most powerful learning experiences were school related. Most are informal learning experiences, such as continuing education courses, museum programs, or church activities. Others are nonformal learning from our day-to-day interactions. What do you think this suggests about designing adult learning experiences?

Relate your powerful learning experience to any professional development that you are currently implementing. How have your participants been affected? As a leader, how can you make sure that others have powerful learning experiences in the professional development you sponsor?

▨ Notes

▨ DAY 16: Balancing Philosophy and Pragmatism

The professional development designer faces many dilemmas and decision points.

—Susan Mundry and Susan Loucks-Horsley

One of the basic polarities within professional development is whether to focus efforts on changing participants' philosophy about something or on pragmatic how-to issues (Mundry & Loucks-Horsley, 1999). As with most polarities, both are essential. However, those who plan or participate in staff development may not see the necessity of integrating the two.

The *philosophical approach* focuses on learning theory and gathering evidence of learning. The *pragmatic approach* emphasizes new materials and practices, such as guides, methods, and curriculum, and other more practical matters.

If a program focuses exclusively on philosophical issues and research on learning, it is likely to ignore the day-to-day reality of making a new program work. If it emphasizes the daily how-to's, it shortchanges learners by focusing excessively on surface elements or the mechanics of doing something new without promoting real change in beliefs and behavior. Obviously, professional development needs both.

How are professional development designers able to be sensitive to both needs?

First, there must be infrastructure that supports a dual approach. Flexibility in scheduling is necessary so participants have time to reflect and interact with their colleagues. Sufficient resources are another requirement for sustaining in-depth learning over time.

Second, a recognition of the need for integrating both the philosophical and pragmatic approaches is necessary. Many participants are more likely to embrace professional development that directly helps them do something specific. On the other hand, they may have to be convinced to delve into the philosophy, research base, or way of thinking that underlies the new approach.

A need can be developed by creating a sense of discomfort or cognitive dissonance (see Day 7). The designers construct experiences that disturb the equilibrium between participants' existing beliefs and practices and the outcomes they get. This can happen through the presentation of data, demonstrations, observations, panel presentations, or a variety of other means.

In planning an appropriate focus for professional development, it is important to do the following:

- Maintain a balance between philosophic and programmatic approaches and be responsive to changing needs in participants and the context.

- Gain agreement among participants about the focus for the professional development and continuously determine whether the focus remains on track as the professional development initiative proceeds.
- Build an infrastructure (funding, schedule, and varied approaches) to support both philosophically and programmatically focused professional development.

▧ Reflection

How do you design for and assess the balance between philosophical and pragmatic matters in the professional development for which you are responsible? Do you see substantially more of one approach than the other? If so, how can you create a better balance?

▧ Notes

▨ DAY 17: Thinking to Learn Versus Learning to Think

Thinking to learn is different from learning to think.

—Charles Thompson and John Zeuli

Is someone playing a word game here? Just exactly what do you mean when you say that thinking to learn is different from learning to think?

Learning to think refers to the acquisition of certain thinking skills that are acquired through instruction and practice. The ability to analyze a piece of written material for evidence of bias is an example of a critical thinking skill. And clearly, learning to think is important. We are not disputing this.

But thinking to learn is different. In implementing a philosophy of thinking to learn, instructors start with what learners already know. They then build a set of experiences that allow learners to assess their current understanding and deepen and broaden it to new levels.

To teach in this manner,

> Teachers need to know how to choose or design problems whose resolution will advance their students' understanding at different points along the developmental pathway toward current disciplinary knowledge, how to help students represent and express their ideas in a variety of ways, how to establish and maintain norms appropriate to a . . . classroom community, and how to orchestrate student discourse. (Thompson & Zeuli, 1999, p. 20)

Through this process, students engage in thinking to learn.

What motivates people who design learning experiences to engage children or adults in "thinking to learn" more than "learning to think"? A major factor is cognitive dissonance. When teachers or instructors observe that what they thought they taught is not exactly what the learners learned, this realization can propel them into reconsideration of their basic ideas about methods. They begin to realize that they cannot "correct" misconceptions simply by saying they are wrong, explaining why, and then presenting the correct information. They begin to appreciate the role of having learners engage with and think through information to develop their own understanding.

In traditional instruction, knowledge is interpreted as facts and skills, teaching as telling, and learning as remembering. In instruction based on thinking to learn, teachers help learners construct their own knowledge, which they are more likely to retain because it has more meaning for them.

▨ Reflection

Think about professional development programs you facilitate or sponsor. Do activities employ a thinking-to-learn approach? If so, how have these activities differed from other, more traditional instruction? Which approach resulted in more learning? How do you know?

How can you promote thinking to learn in professional development programs in your organization? What are specific steps you can take?

▨ Notes

_____

_____

_____

_____

_____

_____

_____

_____

_____

_____

▨ DAY 18: Incorporating Reflexive Practice

It was one of the worst workshops I ever attended. He lectured for three hours on how to use media in presentations.

—A workshop participant

One of the key characteristics of effective professional development is that it is *reflexive*. That means it is true to itself. It is internally consistent in its content and process.

In the instance above, the workshop was not reflexive because the instructor lectured on how to make effective presentations using media. Had he actually used media in his presentation, the session would have been more reflexive. He would have been modeling what he was trying to teach his participants.

Any professional development strategy needs to be reflexive for teachers to the following:

- Take the approach seriously

- See the instructor as credible

- Regard the instruction as practical and real-world oriented

- Explore applications in the classroom

- Have the opportunity to practice new behaviors

Reflexive practice is sometimes confused with reflective practice, another important characteristic of effective professional development. In *reflective practice*, participants have specific times structured into the learning experience to think about what they are learning, its relevance to them, and what they may yet need to learn (just like the reflections in these contemplations). Reflections are important, too, but they shouldn't be confused with reflexive practice.

▨ Reflection

Below are three professional development strategies. For each one, list what it would need to be reflexive. In other words, how would the learning experience be true to itself? (For example, professional development on outdoor education should involve some outdoor activity.)

1. Using various kinds of technology, such as computers, telecommunications, video, and CD-ROMs to learn content and pedagogy

2. Using structured opportunities outside the classroom (courses, seminars, institutes, or workshops) to focus on topics of interest

3. Working one-on-one with teachers in a coaching or mentoring role to improve teaching and learning through a variety of activities

As a leader, how can you make sure that you are being reflexive?

▨ Notes

_____

_____

_____

_____

_____

_____

_____

_____

_____

▨ DAY 19: Equity and Diversity

> *Inequities are a reality of education in the United States.*
> *Acknowledging this fact does not create the problem; it brings*
> *the problem to light so that all . . . can be served. Not in an*
> *identical way, but equitably, with equal opportunity to succeed.*

—Nancy Love

One of the most critical issues that professional developers must consider is equity and diversity. Given the growing minority population in this country and the mobility of our society, understanding and appreciating diversity and being able to respond to it appropriately is an essential adult competency. Equity, in terms of access to professional development, is equally important.

There are normally three concerns related to diversity that need to be addressed in any professional development effort. One relates to the staffing and curriculum of the professional development itself, another to the participants, and the third to the content of the professional development.

Staffing and Curriculum. Is the professional development staff diverse in terms of race/ethnicity, gender, disability, and other factors that may be important to the professional development (e.g., a mix of staff with experience at different grade levels)? Does the staff reflect the diversity within the participant group? Are the content, pedagogy, and materials employed in the professional development free of bias and stereotyping? Does the staff use inclusive language and promote the interaction of all participants?

Participants. What is the racial/ethnic composition of your participant group? Do both women and men participate? Are people with disabilities included? How do you know whether you have met an equity standard regarding the makeup of your participants?

In determining whether you have met an equity standard, there are two possible goals. The first is that the group be represented proportionally to its representation in your organization. For example, if African Americans make up 15 percent of your staff, then they should be approximately 15 percent of your professional development participants. Of course, there must be flexibility in interpreting this guideline, especially with small numbers. That 15 percent could be one person. The distribution of a particular group among grade levels, for example, can also be a factor affecting participation. On the basis of need, you can exceed proportional representation by targeted recruiting.

A second standard is that the participants (if participants are teachers) be proportionally representative of schools that have minority students and/or students with disabilities. Considering the national underrepresentation of minority teachers and teachers with disabilities, this standard may be more appropriate than the first. For example, if Latino students constitute one third of your student population, then about one-third of your participants should teach Latino students. Depending on the needs of the teachers and students, you can also exceed this standard.

Content. This aspect of equity may or may not be applicable to your professional development, depending on its purpose and goals. However, if it addresses teaching of content in any way, these are important considerations. Does the curriculum of your staff development address equity issues in either the content or pedagogy, or both? Here are some possible questions to explore:

- What types of students enroll in the classes the teachers teach? Are they representative of the entire student body? If not, what limits access?

- How do teachers accommodate the diverse learning styles of students?

- Are there instances of bias or stereotyping in the texts or other instructional materials that teachers use? If so, how do teachers use these instances as teaching points? Are there bias-free materials available? If the materials are free of bias, to what extent do they reflect diversity? What types of diversity?

- How does the content affect diverse groups of students? Are there aspects of the content or the pedagogy that might be culturally inappropriate?

- What equity issues exist in assessment? Is one group likely to excel because of some factor or factors, such as bias in the test or testing procedure?

Often, the greatest challenge to diversity is getting people to understand the need for it. They may fail to see the diversity that exists among the different people they work with or how it is going to increase as minority populations grow. Or they may mistakenly believe that being blind to color, race, gender, or disability is desirable. One strategy for dealing with resistance to diversity is to have people wrestle a bit with their perceptions and data about their reality. For example, how aware are they of the ethnic and socioeconomic diversity in their area?

In education, common equity issues focus on when and where the professional development is held, whether teachers in schools in poorer neighborhoods have adequate access to professional development, which teachers get to go, and whether released time and/or compensation are provided.

▨ Reflection

What are the key diversity and equity concerns within your organization? How does your professional development address (or not address) these concerns? What do you think your professional development could do better in dealing with equity and diversity? How can you make that happen?

▨ Notes

_____

_____

_____

_____

_____

_____

_____

_____

_____

▨ DAY 20: Reaching Everyone, or Scaling Up

*A Talented, Dedicated, and Well-Prepared Teacher
in Every Classroom.*

—Title of a publication from the
U.S. Department of Education Teacher Initiative

There are other critical professional development issues that you must not ignore. These include *scaling up*, or reaching everyone, and building a culture for learning.

Who participates in professional development activities? All teachers and staff? Those who volunteer? A smaller number who are hand selected? Who should come?

These are not easy questions to answer.

In the past, one of the usual characteristics of change was that the staff generally had the option of adopting the change or not. Often, they could say, "No, thank you" to the new curriculum or new method. With current reform efforts, there is a much greater focus on scaling up interventions to reach all.

The challenge of scaling up goes beyond providing the same experience to a greater number of participants. We know from the Concerns-Based Adoption Model (CBAM; Hall & Hord, 2000) that people experience different needs surrounding the adoption of an innovation. Providing for all these different needs in a single professional development event is very difficult. The "one size fits all" approach just doesn't work.

Mobility is also a problem. A core group of staff can go through a professional development experience and within a year or two, many of them may be working elsewhere. The result is very uneven implementation of the new program or practices.

What is needed to reach all is an organizational infrastructure and culture that supports a comprehensive and continual intervention. This includes a vision, mission, clear direction, flexibility in scheduling, and adequate resources. There also needs to be a human infrastructure built around a culture of learning and reform, which encourages development of a community of practice. This is how a school culture both encourages and supports the staff to continue learning.

To have a professional development program that affects most people in an organization, planners need to do the following (Mundry & Loucks-Horsley, 1999):

- Collaborate successfully with all staff to have in place an articulated culture for change and supportive policies and practices
- Hold high standards for learning

- Have in place a process for rolling admission so that new or reassigned staff can enroll

▒ Reflection

Is your professional development designed to involve all the staff it needs to reach? What do you need to do to reach others? How can you begin to make changes in organizational infrastructure or human infrastructure to support a totally inclusive staff development program? What steps can you take to encourage the development of a community of practice in your setting?

▒ Notes

_____

_____

_____

_____

_____

_____

_____

_____

_____

▨ DAY 21: Twelve Principles of Knowledge Acquisition

Learning defined as "remembering" is a vestige from the early times of schooling when learning goals were basic literacy and numeracy. . . . Although some information basic to today's goals can be learned through drill and practice, there is a great deal of knowledge that requires a different paradigm of learning— one of building understanding and making connections over time.

—Jill Mirman Owen et al.

Much is known about how people learn. The knowledge base is drawn from research and practice. Here are 12 principles that encompass much of what we know (Owen et al., 1994, pp. 16-29):

1. People are born learners. Notice the natural curiosity of children. All humans are born with an intrinsic motivation to learn.

2. People seek to understand new information and experiences by connecting them to what they already know. New knowledge must be connected to prior knowledge for effective learning to occur.

3. People learn in different ways. Research has documented the fact that people have inclinations toward learning through particular styles or approaches.

4. Thinking about one's own thinking improves performance and the ability to work independently. The ability to stand back and observe one's own thought process is an important skill of effective learners.

5. An individual's stage of intellectual, social, and emotional development affects how he or she learns.

6. Although people may naturally make connections as they learn, they often need help to transfer knowledge or apply it in different contexts. Unconnected knowledge is rarely retained.

7. Having a repertoire of strategies enhances learning. Learning is essentially a process of problem solving. The greater the variety of strategies for achieving a goal that a learner has, the more successful he or she is likely to be.

8. Certain predispositions, attitudes, and habits of mind facilitate learning. Qualities such as flexibility, open-mindedness, reflection, and empathy promote learning. Rigidity, bias, tunnel vision, and impulsiveness are barriers to learning.

9. Working with people who have different learning styles and perspectives enhances learning. Working in a diverse group can stimulate members to engage in higher-order cognitive skills.

10. Those who do the work do the learning. Effective learners create knowledge for themselves, own it, know why they learned it, and how they learned it.

11. A resource-rich environment facilitates learning. For learners to actively construct knowledge, they need access to a wide variety of materials. These include ideas, books, visual and auditory media, technology, artifacts, and opportunities to interact.

12. Developing shared understandings about what constitutes quality work fosters learning. Effective learners integrate their internal goals with external expectations.

▨ Reflection

Reread each of the above principles. As you do so, think about how you have experienced each of these in your life.

Review the principles a second time to look at how each applies to the professional development your organization conducts. Are certain principles well reflected in your organization's professional development? How are they reflected? Are certain principles not being honored? If so, what can you do to make sure all these principles are incorporated into your professional development activities?

▨ Notes

▨ DAY 22: Transferring Situational Learning

Learning is important because no one is born with the ability to function competently as an adult in society.

—National Research Council

Ideally, the learning experiences we engage in apply to real-life situations and help us to be productive workers, be responsible citizens, be competent parents, and have rewarding relationships. Unfortunately, not all our learning experiences enable us to successfully transfer the knowledge to new situations. Some end up being dead-end activities.

What promotes knowledge transfer? What impedes it? The latest research shows the following (National Research Council, 1999):

- Knowledge and skills must be beyond the narrow context in which they are first learned. As an example, knowing how to solve a mathematics problem in school doesn't automatically mean that one can solve similar problems in real life.

- Learners must understand when it is appropriate to apply what they have learned. The conditions of applicability must be made clear; it cannot be assumed that the learner will necessarily see the connection.

- To be widely applicable or transferable, learning must be based on generalized principles. For example, what is learned by rote memory can rarely be transferred. On the other hand, understanding general principles, which can be applied to a variety of situations, promotes transfer.

- Transfer is more likely to occur if learners have conceptual rather than just factual knowledge. For example, conceptual knowledge includes an understanding of part-whole relationships and similarities and differences.

- Individuals who see themselves as both learners and thinkers are better at transfer. They are better able to monitor their own level of understanding and its application. This is essential for becoming a life-long learner.

- Learners need to have sufficient time on task to adequately process information. Learning can't be rushed if the ability to transfer is to develop.

- Prior experiences can help or hinder new learning and, as a result, transfer. Some "unlearning" of misconceptions may have to take place or adjustments made to accommodate for cultural differences.

▨ Reflection

Recall one or two professional development efforts that you have been involved in designing or providing. To what extent did they result in the ability to transfer learning? What was designed into them to ensure that such transfer would occur? What evidence do you have that transfer took place?

▨ Notes

_____

_____

_____

_____

_____

_____

_____

_____

_____

PART V
Teams Learning Together

Historically, professional development in the workplace has focused on individuals' interests and needs. With the advent of teams, there is now a recognition that teams of individuals have certain learning needs that are best met within a team context. The next two contemplations (Days 23–24) explore how teams can learn best together.

▨ DAY 23: Team Learning

*Team learning is not "team building" and shouldn't
be taken on lightly.*

—Peter Senge

As we discovered in Day 10, there are many different strategies for professional development. An emerging strategy for adult learning is job-embedded professional development—that is, learning that occurs within the context of a person's job, often within a team. Leaders need to understand how to set up and support such learning environments.

Although *team building* is a common expression and is well understood, the concept of team learning is relatively new. Traditional team building focuses on improving individual team members' skills as a means for working with each other. It leads to improved communication, contributes to more efficient and effective task performance, and builds stronger relationships among the members.

Team learning is different. It refers to a team's ability to "think and act in new synergistic ways, with full coordination and a sense of unity" (Senge, Roberts, Ross, Smith, & Kleiner, 1994, p. 352). It is about getting a team to function as a whole rather than as a collection of individuals. Team learning begins with a high level of self-knowledge and progresses toward developing understanding of and aligning with other team members. It encompasses the traditional goals of team building but extends far beyond.

The primary approach to team learning is improved conversation through dialogue and skillful discussion. These differ from normal conversation or group discussion in that they follow rules that allow team members to understand and appreciate the different forces at play. Because they don't necessarily come naturally, people need to learn these ways to communicate (Garmston & Wellman, 1999).

For team learning to occur, the following components need to be in place:

- *A task on which to focus and a reason for the group to work together.* This task becomes the practice field on which the team develops.

- *A facilitator to aid learning.* Team members become so engrossed in their own dynamics that there is no way for them to objectively analyze how they are functioning. A trained outside observer who can be impartial is often the best person to facilitate and give feedback.

- *A set of ground rules for their conversation.* For example, teams might develop ground rules that include telling the truth, sharing only pertinent information, limiting airtime, and avoiding blaming statements. There should also be ground rules for making decisions and for handling violations of the ground rules.

These are prerequisites for teams to begin the practice and develop the art of team learning.

▨ Reflection

Think about a team that you are part of. Write down several words that describe how your team currently functions.

Words That Describe My Team. Does your team have a commitment to team learning? What is the evidence? How do you know? If it doesn't, how might you help influence such a choice on your team's part? What do you think your team could accomplish if it focused on team learning?

What My Team Could Accomplish. Does your current focus need to change to make the team learning more effective? How can you help your team move forward? Consider meaningful tasks for all members and processes to guide your work.

▨ Notes

_____

_____

_____

_____

_____

_____

_____

▨ DAY 24: Matching Interventions With Desired Outcomes

The whole is never the sum of its parts—it is greater or lesser, depending on how well the individuals work together.

—Chuck Noll, former coach, Pittsburgh Steelers

Consider the following situation: You are the leader of three newly formed work teams. The teams are responsible for carrying out a specified set of tasks. One team is functioning very well; the other two are having problems determining how to structure themselves to carry out their work. Everyone seems committed to this new way of working, but some people are having more difficulty than others with the following tasks:

- Functioning as a team member rather than as an individual
- Deciding on roles and responsibilities
- Agreeing on a decision-making process
- Disciplining themselves to follow their ground rules and stay on task

Two teams have asked for help. You have reviewed the situation and learned that the members have no experience working in teams. For example, they have never experienced any group decision-making processes. You also find that logistical glitches, such as incompatible software for sharing documents, have become major obstacles to their work.

The key question to consider is this: What response is most likely to address these problems? Will some form of team learning resolve problems, or should the problems be handled differently? Perhaps job restructuring is the answer, different staffing, or reallocation of resources. In the instance above, the incompatible software is primarily a resource or alignment problem. The inexperience of the group in how to function as a team is a team-learning issue.

Below are five different interventions—all of which are forms of professional development. Which of the following do you think would be most appropriate for the teams in question? Least appropriate? Why?

1. Have the two teams watch a video on how to set up and operate effective teams.

2. Bring in an outside consultant to conduct a day of standard team-building activities with the two teams.

3. Have one or two people from the team that is operating well talk to the teams that aren't functioning effectively.

4. Secure an outside consultant to contract with the teams in terms of what they need, conduct observations, and provide feedback and coaching.

5. Send a member of each team that is not working well to observe the more successful team.

Matching the intervention with the desired outcomes is a complex skill. Here are some questions to ask yourself:

- What outcomes am I hoping for?

- Which intervention is most likely to produce the desired outcome?

- Which strategy fits best with the requirements of team learning and the culture of our organization?

- Are resources available to support the preferred strategy?

What is your rationale for your selection of what is most and least appropriate?

▨ Reflection

Think about an ongoing team effort in your organization. Has this team encountered any problems in carrying out its work? If so, what kind of problems? Was an appropriate intervention implemented for the type of problem the team was experiencing?

Has the team experienced any team learning? If so, what? How was it carried out? How successful do you see this effort as being?

As a leader, what can you do to promote the concept of team learning in your organization?

▨ Notes

_____

_____

_____

_____

_____

PART VI
Evaluating Professional Development

The most frequently ignored aspect of professional development is evaluation. Effective leaders need to know what outcomes they can reasonably expect from professional development and have the skill to determine whether the desired results are forthcoming. The next three contemplations (Days 25–27) examine anticipated outcomes, evaluation of professional development, and effective practices in designing and implementing a variety of learning experiences. A fourth contemplation (Day 28) looks at ways to capture and institutionalize the results of evaluations and other lessons learned.

▨ DAY 25: Achieving Desired Outcomes

A program or activity may have great merit and yet be of little worth to the organization simply because it does not coincide with identified needs or is not aligned with the organization's mission.

—Thomas Guskey

How do you know what reasonable outcomes to expect for any professional development program?

Outcomes is a term synonymous with a program's results, effects, or impact. For individuals, outcomes may include changes in knowledge, understanding, attitudes, skills, or practice. For an organization, the outcomes may be evident in changes in policy, goals, operations, or structures.

Sometimes, distinctions are made among short-term, intermediate, and long-term outcomes to designate when a particular outcome is expected to appear. Achieving intermediate and long-term outcomes is always more difficult because of the interaction between the program and its environment. There can be numerous intervening variables that can support, reduce, or nullify the anticipated outcomes.

One of the most common flaws of professional development planning and implementation is overestimating the magnitude and number of outcomes. In most cases, acquiring new knowledge and skills and changing attitudes and behaviors require a sustained intervention. Having an impact on services or products requires even more time and effort. And regardless of how good a program is, the intervening environmental factors influence the outcomes—most often in a negative way (Kaser & Bourexis, 1999).

▨ Reflection

Think of a professional development program going on in your organization. It may be a single event or a sustained activity. What are the anticipated outcomes? For each anticipated outcome, ask yourself the following questions:

- Is the outcome best described as short-term, intermediate, or long-term?

- Is the outcome realistic in light of the intervention? How do you know?

- Is the outcome measurable? How would you know whether you had achieved it?

What is the relationship among the outcomes? Are they of one type or a mix? What is your overall assessment of the anticipated outcomes of your professional development program? Do you need to make some adjustments? If so, how will you do this?

▧ Notes

_____

_____

_____

_____

_____

_____

_____

_____

_____

_____

▧ DAY 26: Gathering Evaluation Data

*Two large issues must be addressed if . . . evaluation challenges
are to be met successfully: (a) the quality of staff development
and (b) the types of evidence of effectiveness that policymakers
and school leaders require.*

—Dennis Sparks

Leaders are accountable for results. Leaders who promote learning in the
workplace need to assess what the learning is and how relevant and transferable it is to the mission of the organization.

As a leader, what information do you want to know about the value of different learning experiences?

- Was the professional development based on effective practice? Was a
  needs assessment conducted? Were learner characteristics taken into
  account? Was the program designed and conducted according to effective practice? Was the program carried out according to plan?

- What did the participants think of the professional development? Did
  they learn what they expected to learn? Was the experience worthwhile? Were the logistics handled properly? Do they expect the experience to change their attitudes and behavior?

- Did the participants learn anything? Did they gain new knowledge
  and/or acquire new skills?

- Did the professional development change participants' behavior?
  What did the participants do differently as a result of the professional
  development they experienced? Did their attitudes and/or behavior
  change?

- What were the ultimate outcomes of the professional development?
  Was there an improvement in either services or products as a result of
  the experience (e.g., enhanced student achievement)?

There are degrees of difficulty in gathering data to answer these five very
different questions. It is easiest to determine what participants think about a
professional development experience. It is infinitely more difficult—also
more time-consuming and expensive—to determine whether the professional
development eventually improves knowledge and skills and adds value to the
services or products that participants provide.

▧ Reflection

Think of some professional development program that your organization
is involved in. Next, determine what you would want to know if you were

evaluating this professional development. You can use the above questions to guide what you want to find out. Write down what you want to evaluate in the space below.

Below are several common ways of gathering evaluation data. Match the data-gathering technique with what you want to find out. In each instance, ask yourself whether what you have listed will produce the best data in the most efficient and cost-effective way.

Data-gathering techniques: individual or group interview, pre- or post-survey, case study, post-event rating sheet, self-report assessment of attitude or behavioral change, third-party observation, analysis of journals or other written material.

Which of these offers the greatest potential for your situation? What will it take in terms of time and cost?

▨ Notes

_____

_____

_____

_____

_____

_____

_____

_____

▨ DAY 27: Identifying Key Features of Successful Programs

Over the years, a lot of good things have been done in the name of professional development. So have a lot of rotten things. What professional developers have not done is provide evidence to document the difference between the good and the rotten.

—Thomas Guskey

Think about a worthwhile professional development experience you have been part of and one that you thought was a waste of your time. Jot down some of the characteristics of each in the columns below:

An Effective Experience   An Ineffective Experience

_____   _____

_____   _____

_____   _____

_____   _____

_____   _____

When you compare what you have written in the two columns, you will probably see that some standard characteristics contribute to making any professional development program successful. Some approaches also undermine the success of such a venture.

There is a growing body of literature about the key features of successful professional development programs (Kaser & Bourexis, 1999; Stiles, Loucks-Horsley, & Hewson, 1998). These are components that must be in place to ensure that a program is designed for quality from the onset.

These components have been identified from research and from the experience of seasoned practitioners. If the components are not firmly in place, the program may not go well and will not have the impact desired. Attending to these components increases the likelihood of the desired impact.

The major components of professional development include a vision of what the teacher does as a result of the experience, program activities, the unique contribution of the host organization, follow-up, teacher leadership and responsibility, systemic connections, program administration, and evaluation. Each component has several descriptors. For example, here are descriptors of two teacher development program activities: (a) model teaching principles and strategies that can be transferred to the classroom and (b) include opportunities to practice new classroom behaviors or strategies.

One approach to designing solid programs is knowing *best practice* (e.g., the necessity for follow-up support and practice) and planning a program accordingly. By using a discrepancy model, it is possible to compare best practice with the design of the program as well as its implementation, while looking for areas of congruence as well as discrepancy. This approach is often used for formative evaluation but can also be used for summative or outcome evaluation. The use of best practice offers professional developers a variety of ways of ensuring quality programs (Kaser et al., 1999).

◼ Reflection

Think of a professional development program in your organization. Jot down what you think the best practice would be for that program. How can you confirm your answers? How can you begin to use best practice in designing, conducting, and evaluating your program?

◼ Notes

▨ DAY 28: Capturing Lessons Learned

A great cartoon in The New Yorker *some years back showed two venerable men, obviously scientists, sitting back to back at their respective desks. One says to the other, "It's just come to my attention that we've both been working on the same problem for the last twenty-five years."*

—Nancy M. Dixon

One of the ways to institutionalize lifelong learning is for an organization to *capture lessons learned.* Lessons learned are key organizational learnings—documentation of what works and does not work in a field—captured over the years. The lessons learned can come from research and evaluation efforts, action research, the work of experienced practitioners, or the day-to-day experience of the staff carrying out their jobs.

Often, the collective lessons learned in an organization are not documented and shared. Reorganization and staff reassignment or turnover can disperse those who possess institutional memory. Under time constraints, the staff may not seek out those with more experience. New staff members may not be sufficiently oriented toward the organization's way of doing work.

Here is the way capturing lessons learned can work. Imagine that you are responsible for providing new staff orientation each fall. Over the years, you have kept a lessons-learned file that has several headings. One heading is Scheduling and Logistics. Another is Staff Benefits. Another is Content, subdivided by subject (e.g., District Disciplinary Policies and Procedures, Classroom Management, District Standards, Parent Involvement, Multicultural Issues, etc.)

A staff member who is responsible for setting up the orientation checks the Scheduling and Logistics file. There, he or she finds some valuable pieces of information: The facility you normally use is currently under renovation and is not available; in previous sessions, the staff preferred starting at 8:00 rather than 9:00 in the morning so they could get out early; Chef du Jour has consistently provided the best food at the lowest price. Each file has similar information about what has and hasn't worked in the past—valuable information to those planning the orientation, especially those who are new to this function themselves. All files are electronic and are updated after each new orientation.

▨ Reflection

In your current role, are you capturing lessons learned? If so, how? Are they being used?

If you are not capturing lessons learned, how might you do so? What would your process look like? How would you be sure that your staff checks lessons learned before undertaking a task?

▧ Notes

PART VII
Modeling Expertise

Are there specific characteristics that define experts? If you are an expert, what are your areas of expertise? How do leaders effectively model lifelong learning, and what is the importance of doing so? The contemplations conclude with a 10-step approach to acquiring new knowledge, skills, or competencies.

▨ DAY 29: Defining Expertise

Understanding expertise is important because it provides insights into the nature of thinking and problem solving.

—National Research Council

Effective leaders have expertise. But what is an *expert*? Is it a general term used to describe someone who knows a lot about a specific subject? Exactly what makes someone an expert? Is there a line that one crosses to move into expertise?

Interestingly, recent research has revealed clear distinctions between novices and experts. Expertise is not just the possession of general abilities, such as memory or intelligence, nor is it the use of general strategies. Instead, experts have extensive knowledge that affects their perceptions and how they process information. This affects what they remember, how they reason, and how they solve problems—all very important attributes of leaders.

Recent research shows the following (National Research Council, 1999, p. xiii):

- Experts notice features and meaningful patterns of information that novices don't detect.

- Experts have acquired a great deal of content knowledge that is highly organized. Their organization of information reflects a deep understanding of the subject matter.

- Experts' knowledge cannot be reduced to sets of isolated facts or propositions, but instead, reflects contexts of applicability—it is "conditionalized."

- Experts are able to retrieve important aspects of their knowledge with little effort.

- Though experts know their disciplines thoroughly, this does not guarantee that they are able to instruct others about the topic.

- Experts have varying levels of flexibility in their approaches to new situations.

What are some of the implications of these findings?

All learners can profit from practice with identifying patterns, understanding problems in terms of underlying concepts or big ideas, using models of how experts approach and solve problems, recognizing relevant versus irrelevant information, determining conditions under which information is important, and being able to retrieve the right information with ease. These are skills that differentiate the expert from the person who is competent from the novice.

▨ Reflection

Do you consider yourself an expert in one or more areas? If so, to what extent do these research findings apply to you? Do you see yourself as needing additional knowledge and/or skills to become an expert?

If you want to grow in your expertise, what steps can you take?

Does your organization recognize the value of experts and encourage the development of expertise? As a leader, what can you do to help others in your organization develop expertise?

▨ Notes

_____

_____

_____

_____

_____

_____

_____

_____

_____

▨ DAY 30: Modeling Lifelong Learning

*Learning as a way of being is a whole mentality. It is a way
of being in the world. . . . Learning as a way of being is a whole
posture toward experience, a way of framing or interpreting
all experience as a learning opportunity.*

—Peter B. Vaill

An organization is committed to lifelong learning insofar as its leaders model continuous learning themselves, along with having organizational policies and procedures that support lifelong learning for all employees.

Such policies represent an organizational commitment to investing in human capital and being a learning organization in all aspects. This covers a range of topics, starting with a philosophical statement on individual, team, and organizational learning, to specifics such as employees taking reflection time for themselves; orientation for all new and newly promoted employees; and the sources and financial support for ongoing learning.

Regardless of what any written policy says, the behavior of the leaders of an organization is the most important yardstick for determining what an organization truly values. If the policy says one thing and the leader does another, the stronger message comes from the leader's actions.

Here is what you as a leader can do to model lifelong learning:

1. Say you don't know when you don't know; don't pretend to have all the answers.

2 Listen attentively and be open to what others have to say.

3. Regularly seek out the opinions of others.

4. When challenged, listen carefully and deal with the facts; try not to be defensive.

5. Insist that all new and newly promoted employees go through orientation; do so yourself, if and when that is applicable. Know what the orientation of your staff entails and discuss that with them, as appropriate.

6. Set aside reflection time for yourself and expect your staff to do the same. Also schedule reflection time for your group or team.

7. Read and share what you read with others, as appropriate.

8. Have learning goals for yourself and let others know what these are.

9. Attend conferences in your field and encourage others to do the same.

10. Support quality professional development for your staff and others in your organization.

11. See mistakes and failures as opportunities to learn.

12. Value staying on top of research in your field.

13. Value expertise and use experts.

14. Adopt a "problems are our friends" orientation.

15. Subscribe to a philosophy of personal mastery.

Your adherence to these actions will convey your commitment to learning and to learning as a way of being.

▨ Reflection

Reread the above list and check off those behaviors that currently describe you in relation to lifelong learning.

How many and which ones did you check? How strong is your commitment to lifelong learning for yourself and for your organization? If you believe that it needs to be strengthened, what can you do? How can you help others demonstrate lifelong learning behaviors?

▨ Notes

_____

_____

_____

_____

_____

_____

_____

▧ DAY 31: Ten-Step Plan for Lifelong Learning

*Look at the need to learn something new as an opportunity
rather than a burden.*

—Don Horsley

It used to be that leaders were hired for what they knew. Nowadays, they are more likely to be hired for their speed of learning.

Those who are leaders (and those who aspire to be leaders) are more likely to be successful if they take responsibility for their continuous learning and can learn quickly.

Here is a 10-step plan to guide you in approaching your own lifelong learning and, in the process, flatten your learning curve (Reynolds, 2000).

1. *Acknowledge what you want to learn and why you want to learn it.* Sometimes, you want to learn something because it is new, exciting, and offers certain benefits. Other times, you decide to learn something because you realize that you need to know it. To get to this place, you may need to work through some denial and acknowledge that you must obtain certain knowledge and skills that you don't currently have.

2. *Identify any negative feelings you have about learning something new.* Perhaps you are lucky to feel only excitement and anticipation about learning what you have chosen to learn. However, adults often enter a new learning experience with negative feelings. Are there any barriers that may keep you from acquiring the knowledge and skills you want? Are you afraid that you don't have the ability, the time, or the resources to learn what you have decided to learn? Do you worry about being perceived as incompetent or feeling uncomfortable as you learn something new? Simply voicing these feelings or talking them through with someone else can help to dispel them.

3. *Determine your motivation for learning something new.* Your motivation for learning influences your persistence and ultimately your success. Is there external pressure? Are you motivated by an internal desire? Perhaps both? Together, an internal desire and an external demand provide the strongest motivation.

4. *Make a conscious choice to learn what it is that you want.* You need to say to yourself or out loud, "Within the next six months, I choose to learn. . . ." Making a conscious choice is much more powerful than simply saying, "Gee, I'd really like to learn . . . someday."

5. *To move forward, be prepared to give up your attachment to the old way of doing things.* We often are attached to the past. Giving up that attachment may be necessary before we can move on to learn some-

thing new. It may even be necessary to grieve the loss of the old be-fore we can move on to the new.

6. *Back up your choice with a plan.* How do you learn best? How much time do you have to acquire new knowledge or skills? What re-sources do you need? Do you have them, or where can you get hold of them? Your answers to these questions are the core of an action plan to guide your learning.

7. *Establish some success criteria for yourself.* How will you know whether you are making progress or when you have reached your goal? Establishing one or two benchmarks can help you gauge your progress.

8. *Build in rewards for yourself.* Rewards are highly individualized, so pick your own. Maybe it is intrinsic—for example, simply complet-ing your plan. Maybe it is extrinsic—for example, giving yourself a treat, such as a weekend away.

9. *Recognize that how you go about learning is an act of symbolic leadership that will not go unnoticed.* Others will observe how you approach lifelong learning and will learn from your behavior. You are a role model even though you may not be aware of it.

10. *Keep learning.* There is no end, and the pace is likely to quicken rather than slow down.

▨ Reflection

This book presents different aspects of learning and asks you to reflect on each. In addition, Day 30 lists a variety of actions that you, as a leader, can take to model lifelong learning. Review the contemplations and select some-thing that you need to understand or do better. Develop a plan for learning using the 10 actions listed above. To work on flattening your learning curve, consider a time frame that is shorter than what you would normally lay out for yourself.

▨ Notes

_____

_____

_____

Bibliography

Alvarado, A. (1998). Professional development is the job. *American Educator, 18,* 18-23.

Bolman, L. G., & Deal, T. E. (1991). *Reframing organizations: Artistry, choice, and leadership.* San Francisco: Jossey-Bass.

Dixon, N. M. (2000). *Common knowledge: How companies thrive by sharing what they know.* Boston: Harvard Business School Press.

Garmston, R. J., & Wellman, B. M. (1999). *The adaptive school: A sourcebook for developing collaborative groups.* Norwood, MA: Christopher-Gordon.

Guskey, T. (2000). *Evaluating professional development.* Thousand Oaks, CA: Corwin.

Hall, G., & Hord, S. (2000). *Implementing change: Patterns, principles, and potholes.* Needham Heights, MA: Allyn & Bacon.

Kaser, J. S., & Bourexis, P. S. (with Loucks-Horsley, S., & Raizen, S. A.). (1999). *Enhancing program quality in science and mathematics.* Thousand Oaks, CA: Corwin.

Lawrence, G. (1993). *People types and tiger stripes.* Gainesville, FL: Center for Applications of Psychological Type.

Lewin, K. (1946). Action research and minority problems. *Journal of Social Issues, 2,* 34-46.

Lieberman, A., & Miller, L. (2000). Teaching and teaching development: A new synthesis for a new century. In R. Brandt, (Ed.), *Education in a new era.* Alexandria, VA: Association for Supervision and Curriculum Development.

Loucks-Horsley, S., Hewson, P. W., Love, N., & Stiles, K. E. (1998). *Designing professional development for teachers of science and mathematics.* Thousand Oaks, CA: Corwin.

Love, N. (2001). *Using data—Getting results.* Cambridge, MA: Regional Alliance for Mathematics and Science Education Reform.

Mundry, S., & Loucks-Horsley, S. (1999, April). Designing professional development for science and mathematics teachers: Decision points and dilemmas. *NISE Brief, 3.* Available on the World Wide Web at: wcer.wisc.edu/NISE/publications/briefs

National Research Council. (1999). *How people learn: Brain, mind, experience, and school.* Washington, DC: National Academy Press.

Owen, J. M., Cox, P. L., & Watkins, J. (1994). *Genuine reward: Community inquiry into connecting learning, teaching, and assessing.* Andover, MA: The Regional Laboratory for Educational Improvement of the Northeast and Islands.

Peters, T. (1987). *Thriving on chaos: Handbook for a management revolution.* New York: Knopf.

Reynolds, L. (2000, August 11). *Continuous learning skills critical to career success in new economy.* Available on the World Wide Web at: Kaplancollege.com

Senge, P. M. (1990). *The fifth discipline.* New York: Doubleday.

Senge, P. M., Roberts, C., Ross, R. B., Smith, B. J., & Kleiner, A. (1994). *The fifth discipline fieldbook.* New York: Doubleday.

Sparks, D., & Hirsch, S. (1997). *A new vision for staff development.* Alexandria, VA: Association for Supervision and Curriculum Development; Oxford, OH: National Staff Development Council.

Stiles, K., Loucks-Horsley, S., & Hewson, P. (1998). Principles of effective professional development for mathematics and science education: A synthesis of standards. *NISE Brief, 1.* (Reprinted 1999, August.) Available on the World Wide Web at: wcer.wisc.edu/NISE/publications/briefs

Thompson, C., & Zeuli, J. (1999). The frame and tapestry: Standards-based reform and professional development. In L. Darling-Hammond & G. Sykes (Eds.), *Heart of the matter: Teaching as the learning profession.* San Francisco: Jossey-Bass.

U.S. Department of Education Initiative on Teaching. (n.d.). *A talented, dedicated, and well-prepared teacher in every classroom.* Washington, DC: U.S. Department of Education.

Vaill, P. B. (1996). *Learning as a way of being.* San Francisco: Jossey-Bass.

Book Four

▧ Leading Effective Groups

More and more leaders find themselves working with groups. The groups may be refining a mission statement, shoring up a staff recruiting program, or learning about new standards. Whatever its purpose, the group is usually more effective when led by someone with good presentation and facilitation skills. As organizations increasingly use teams to carry out work, leaders must apply the new skill of helping to facilitate effective team learning and performance.

The kind of group we address in this book meets over a period of time. Such groups have something to learn, issues to address, studies to conduct, tasks to complete, or problems to solve. Although much of what we say also applies to groups that meet just once or twice, our major focus is on leaders and their ongoing groups.

We ask questions: What are different roles for leaders in groups? How do leaders behave in these different roles? How do people in groups talk to one another to ensure effective outcomes? For example, what is the difference between dialogue and discussion, and when should each be used?

How does one plan and conduct successful meetings? What are the key components of successful meetings? How does a group handle decision making, when is consensus necessary, and when will a simple majority suffice? How does a group handle conflict effectively? Monitor participation? Give and receive negative feedback? And finally, how should a group evolve over time?

The content of the 31 contemplations in this book concerns best practice in leading groups. The contemplations are divided into two parts. Part I addresses how people in groups talk with one another. Part II discusses how effective groups function. The focus is always on the leader's role in helping to improve group communication and effectiveness.

PART I

Developing a Community Environment

The goal of all groups, if they are to carry out their mission effectively and efficiently, is to develop community. According to Palmer (1998, p. 90), "Community is an outward and visible sign of an inward and invisible grace, the flowing of personal identity and integrity into the world of relationships." The leader's role is to build an efficacious environment so that teams can do their work in a culture of respect and continuous improvement.

One component of community flows from the way group members talk among themselves and to others outside their group. "Good talk" does not just happen. It is the result of individuals developing skills and agreeing that they want to interact with each other in very specific ways.

The first contemplation (Day 1) outlines the four roles of group leaders, all of which are applicable by the audience of this book. The next nine contemplations (Days 2–10) present a series of interrelated norms on how people in groups can best talk to each other and, in that process, build community. The next two (Days 11–12) explore two very different ways of talking—dialogue and discussion—and the appropriate use of each to further group growth, development, and productivity.

▨ DAY 1: Four Roles of Group Leaders

Good leaders make people feel that they're at the very heart of things, not at the periphery. Everyone feels that he or she makes a difference to the success of the organization. When that happens, people feel centered and that gives their work meaning.

—Warren Bennis

What exactly is a group leader? Does this person actually direct the group's work? Help the group with its process? Intervene only when the group has problems?

The answer is, "that depends." Leaders have different roles in groups. Effective leaders know how to select and execute the right role for the right group and when and how to switch roles within a group.

The following are brief descriptions of each of the four most common roles for group leaders (Garmston & Wellman, 1999, pp. 27-28).

Facilitator. Being a facilitator is an appropriate role when the group's purpose is dialogue, shared decision making, solving a problem, or planning. The facilitator's role is to manage the process. He or she keeps the group on task, making sure that it does what it is supposed to do. This person is not the authority or expert and stays out of the content of the task, usually focusing only on the process.

Presenter. The role of presenters is to teach. A person in this role works with a group to broaden its knowledge, skills, or attitudes. A presenter can—and should—use a variety of instructional techniques and actively involve group members in their own learning.

Coach. Coaches help others achieve their own goals. At the same time, the coach helps colleagues strengthen their knowledge and skills in areas where they need guidance. Like the facilitator, the coach has a role that is nonjudgmental.

Consultant. The role of consultants is to provide their expertise to a group. Consultants target the content, process, or both, to help the group achieve its goals. To be effective in this role, the consultant must be trusted by the group and keep the desired outcomes foremost in mind.

▨ Reflection

Think of the group or groups that you work with. For each group, what role do you play? Does your role match the needs and purposes of the group?

Is this role the most appropriate one for you? Are group members clear about your role? How do you know?

Which of the four roles are you most comfortable with? Least comfortable with?

If you need to strengthen your skills in one of the roles, which one would that be? How can you increase your effectiveness? (One way is to focus specifically on the topics in this chapter that will be helpful to you.)

▨ Notes

▨ DAY 2: Group Norms of Collaboration

Many people dislike meetings, but meetings don't have to be disliked. As in other processes, they can be studied and constantly improved.

—From *The Team Handbook*, Peter R. Scholtes et al.

Effective groups establish and follow certain ways of functioning, which we call *norms*.

Different groups have different norms. Some may focus on how the group uses time, the roles members may play, or the conditions under which the group meets.

To have the kind of productive and collaborative groups we address in this chapter, group members must embrace certain norms. Garmston and Wellman (1999) have identified seven norms essential for collaborative work. They call them "norms" rather than "skills" because they see the actions as behaviors that *all* group members use. Thus, the behavior becomes normative, or basic, to group functioning. When these norms become second nature to groups, "cohesion, energy, and commitment to shared work and to the group increase dramatically" (Garmston & Wellman, 1999, p. 37), and a community exists.

The following norms address ways people talk to one another:

- Pausing

- Paraphrasing

- Probing for specificity

- Putting ideas on the table

- Paying attention to self and others

- Presuming positive intentions

- Pursuing a balance between advocacy and inquiry

Underlying these norms is an explicit intention to support the work that needs to be done and to develop the group and the communication skills of group members.

Garmston and Wellman (1999) suggest that regardless of the role a leader has in a group (facilitator, presenter, coach, or consultant), it is important that he or she model these seven norms of collaboration. If the leader is skillful in adhering to the norms, other group members are likely to do the same. And if current group members model the desired behavior, new group members will follow suit.

▨ Reflection

Think about a group, or groups, that you have been part of. Did any of these groups have a set of agreed-upon norms that supported their work? What were these norms? Were any of them similar to the ones listed above? What differences did you see between groups that had agreed on a common set of norms and those that didn't? How would you describe the differences?

Are there groups that you are part of now that could benefit from establishing shared norms? If so, how can you help this group? What types of norms would be most helpful to them in meeting their group goals?

▨ Notes

_____

_____

_____

_____

_____

_____

_____

_____

_____

▨ DAY 3: Group Norm #1–Pausing

I have often regretted my speech, but never my silence.

—Xenocrates

▨ Pausing

Group members, including leaders, are often so intent on what they are going to say next that they either aren't listening or fail to give themselves and others adequate processing time.

Garmston and Wellman (1999) point out that a speaker's pausing, or providing wait time, is essential so that others can process and respond to what has been said. It also gives you as group leader the opportunity to reword in your own mind what others say to further understand their perspective.

People who are introverted normally require more processing time. They internally process what has been said. Those who are more extraverted tend to process externally. They are the people who say, "I really don't know what I think until the words start coming out of my mouth." The introvert is more inclined to comment, "I need some time to think about that." Keeping a balance so that introverts have sufficient processing time and extraverts do not get impatient or bored is a challenge for a group and its leader.

Key aspects of pausing include the following (Garmston & Wellman, 1998, chap. 3):

- Paying close attention to what others are saying

- Allowing processing time after a comment or question so that all group members have the opportunity to think through what has just been said

- Rewording in one's own mind what is being said

- Timing comments and questions so they are appropriately placed in the group interaction

▨ Reflection

Here is a brief segment of a group interaction. Read the exchanges and answer the questions at the end.

Group Leader:　One of the criteria that we have to decide in setting up this scholarship program is, given our pool of money, how many scholarships do we want to award? Do we want to give several deserving students smaller amounts of money, or would we rather give larger amounts to just two or three students? In making this decision, we need to keep in mind other possible sources of scholarships, grants, or loans that our applicants may have available to them. Along with that, we need to consider our purpose—that is, to support minority students who want to become mathematics or science teachers.

Group Member A: I think that we need to—

Group Leader: Excuse me, Group Member A, can we all take a few moments to jot down our thoughts about this before starting to interact? This is a very important decision we're about to make, and we want everyone's best thinking.

Group Leader: (After a couple of minutes) Okay, Group Member A, what are your thoughts?

Group Member A: I think that we need to give smaller amounts to up to 10 students. Investing all our money in just 2 or 3 students is too risky. We have no guarantees that they will actually continue with mathematics or science or go into teaching.

Group Member B: I think you're absolutely right. It's better to spread the money around.

Group Member C: I disagree. Our applicants deserve more support—

Group Member D: Yeah, you're absolutely right. The more support we give them, the more likely they'll stay the course and become mathematics or science teachers. Diluting our effort may deter them. There are no guarantees. Let's pick the best students and give them more support.

Group Member E: What kind of application do you think they should fill out?

Group Member A: I have a sample in my office. Would you like me to get it so we all can look at it?

Group Leader: Can we hold off on that topic for a bit and go back to our original topic of how many scholarships we want to give at what level? Group Members A and D seem to have captured the two perspectives. Can each of you be more specific by suggesting how many scholarships at what level you think would be appropriate?

Questions:

1. Where do you see the group leader honoring the norm of pausing to facilitate group interaction?

2. What are examples in which the group leader does not use the norm of pausing?

3. If you were the leader of this group, what would you have done differently and why?

▧ Notes

▨ DAY 4: Group Norm #2–Paraphrasing

What we've got here is failure to communicate.

—*Cool Hand Luke* (screenplay)

▨ Paraphrasing

Paraphrasing is a norm that Garmston and Wellman (1999) see as essential for group understanding. It is a restatement of something that has been said. The technique is important for the following reasons:

- It enables a speaker to know whether he or she was heard correctly.

- It honors the worth of group members by recognizing the content and emotion of their contributions.

- It moves the interaction forward through synthesizing or summarizing.

- It allows for correction of any vagueness, lack of clarity, or imprecision.

- It sets the stage for probing for details and elaboration.

Paraphrasing says to the speaker that you are listening, that you are attempting to understand, and that you care.

There is a logical flow to paraphrasing. First, signal your intent to paraphrase. Paraphrases should begin with "you" rather than "I" to keep the focus on the group member. For example: "You're suggesting that the group . . ." rather than "I hear you say that the group. . . ." Other possible stems include, "You're thinking . . . ," "You're wanting . . . , or "Am I understanding you to . . . ?"

Next, choose a logical level with which to respond. There are three such levels (Garmston & Wellman, 1999, p. 41):

1. Acknowledging and clarifying the speaker's content and emotion

2. Summarizing by organizing and synthesizing discussion or by identifying themes

3. Shifting focus to a higher or lower logical level. Going to a higher level happens when the listener connects what he or she has heard with conceptual ideas, such as goals, assumptions, or values. Going to a lower level happens when the listener anchors abstractions in the concrete by providing specific details he or she has heard.

Paraphrasing that summarizes or shifts the logical level of discourse can both support and challenge group members.

▨ Reflection

Here are five statements made by members in a group that you are leading. How would you paraphrase each one to honor the group member's content and emotion, to summarize discussion or identify themes, or to raise or lower the logical level of the discourse?

To help you get started, here is an example that paraphrases the speaker's content and emotion:

The comment: "I'm frustrated and angry. I spent two days preparing this report for our meeting, and no one has even read it. What kind of support is that? When last we met, you all were adamant about my having this report to you ASAP. What happened?"

The paraphrase: "You're obviously upset and rightly so. You've rearranged your schedule to get this report to us, as per our request, and none of us has read it. Your concerns are legitimate. Can we take a few minutes to figure out what happened?"

Remember to start with *you* rather than *I*:

Example A: "I don't think this group is following its own norms."

Example B: "They won't like it if we decide to hold the professional development the third week of August."

Example C: "I think this curriculum is so much better than the one we're currently using."

Example D: "Implementing this new curriculum will be a breeze. Nobody will have any problems with it."

Example E: "I disagree."

▨ Notes

_____

_____

_____

_____

▨ DAY 5: Group Norm #3–Probing

The important thing is not to stop questioning.

—Albert Einstein

▨ Probing

As human beings, our utterances are not always complete and clear. In our interactions, we often need to probe, for a number of different reasons. We may seek data, information, or knowledge; or opinions, feelings, or commitments. We may also be looking for clarity, details, personal connections, past experiences, values, beliefs, or any number of other things.

The danger with probing is that it can often be seen as interrogation. Think back to when you were a child and a parent found evidence that you had done something wrong. Recall the string of questions hurled at you: "What time did you get home? Where were you? Who were you with? Why didn't you call?" Our probing of others can have a similar tone. At the same time, our questions are legitimate and move interaction forward.

One way of neutralizing the interrogation aspect of probing is by paraphrasing first (Garmston & Wellman, 1999). As you learned in Norm #2, start by using "you" instead of "I" so that you honor the person's content and emotion. This sets the stage for asking a probing question without being so threatening. Here is an example:

Without paraphrasing: "Why do you think that no new staff should serve on the district-wide committee? I think they bring a new perspective."

With paraphrasing: "So, you're thinking that we should remove all new staff from the group. Can you say more about how you came to that conclusion?"

What difference do you see between these two examples?

Another reason for probing is our human tendency to rely on generalizations, deletions, and distortions in our communication. These typical behaviors can lead to vagueness and lack of clarity. Comments such as the following are commonplace:

- "Do they have any there?"

- "I want to negotiate that with him."

- "That was the best meeting the committee has ever had."

- "Everyone knows that we tried that, and it didn't work."

So, what is the source of the vagueness? In the first example, the lack of clarity regarding "they," "any," and "there." In the second example, just what does "negotiate" mean? What does "that" refer to, and who is the person? And what is "best" about the meeting in the third example? And finally, who is "everyone"?

▨ Reflection

Here are the examples used for Norm #2. This time, take your paraphrase and add a question that seeks additional information that would move your group interaction forward. If you need help, here are some possible lead-in lines: "You're suggesting or recommending . . . ," "You seem to be thinking that . . . or wondering about . . . ," or "From your perspective, it looks as if. . . ."

Example A: "I don't think this group is following its own norms."

Example B: "They won't like it if we decide to hold the professional development the third week of August."

Example C: "I think this curriculum is so much better than the one we're currently using."

Example D: "Implementing this new curriculum will be a breeze. Nobody will have any problems with it."

Example E: "I disagree."

Now, go back and review your responses. Are they more likely to be perceived as interrogation with or without the paraphrasing? How do you know?

Here are some examples of lack of clarity in language. Can you identify the vagueness? How would you restate the sentence for greater specificity?

- "What we need is more professional development."
- "We're working to improve our faculty/staff morale."
- "Our midlevel managers just aren't meeting their production schedules."
- "All children can learn."

▨ Notes

_____

_____

_____

▧ DAY 6: Group Norm #4–Putting Ideas on the Table or Pulling Them Off

Good questions outrank easy answers.

—Paul Samuelson

▧ Putting Ideas on the Table or Pulling Them Off

The ideas that we contribute to group interaction are what moves a group forward or backward (Garmston & Wellman, 1999).

Whenever we put out an idea, we want it considered because of its own merits, not because we ourselves are advocating the idea. (Advocacy comes later; see Day 10.) This is important because group members tend to react to ideas on the basis of their relationships with and opinion of the speaker, rather than on the merits of the idea itself. To separate ourselves from our ideas, we label them as *thoughts* and *suggestions*—for group consideration, not for personal advocacy.

Here is an example of how to introduce an idea. Declare your intention of presenting a suggestion to simply move the group thinking forward: "Here is one way that we might approach resolving the conflict we're facing." Another approach: "Here is a thought. How about postponing the conference until after the holiday so that . . . ?" Notice that this approach puts some distance between you and your suggestion so that it can be considered on its own value, independent of your status or position within the group.

Before putting an idea on the table, it is a good idea to ask yourself whether your contribution is relevant to the topic under discussion, and if it will move your group forward.

The flip side of putting an idea on the table is taking it off. We do that when we have put forth a suggestion that no longer seems feasible or is blocking the group in some way. By removing your inappropriate contribution, you take responsibility for your role in carrying out the group's work. And taking items off is easy—as long as you are not attached to your suggestion: "This clearly isn't a workable idea. Let's scrap it and move on to something else."

▧ Reflection

Here is one scenario: The group you are leading is exploring ways to get 95 percent of the elementary teachers to participate in a series of professional development workshops on assessment. As the discussion moves along, you find you have the following to contribute:

- Prior experience in getting almost all teachers to participate in a professional development program

- An idea on how to motivate teachers to participate under this set of circumstances

Write down the way you might state your contributions so the group is likely to consider them on their own merit rather than because you as the leader suggested them.

A second scenario: In this group interaction, one member contributes two or three ideas and starts advocating one of them at the time, while the group is still generating ideas rather than evaluating them. What would you do to keep brainstorming ideas before moving on to considering their pros and cons?

▨ Notes

_____

_____

_____

_____

_____

_____

_____

_____

_____

▧ DAY 7: Group Norm #5– Paying Attention to Self and Others, Verbal Communication

Many attempts to communicate are nullified by saying too much.

—Robert Greenleaf

▧ Paying Attention to Self and Others, Verbal Communication

Being attentive to both verbal and nonverbal communication from oneself and other group members is another key to effective group interaction (Garmston & Wellman, 1999).

By paying attention to the physical and verbal cues in ourselves and others, we are able to do the following:

- Spot differences in people's beliefs, values, and communication styles

- See things from a variety of perspectives

- Use the nonverbal behavior of others to modify our own behavior

Attending to your own verbal and nonverbal behavior and that of others underlies all the norms. All seven are interactive and synergistic rather than existing in isolation. For example, when you paraphrase, you are paying attention to others and checking your own understanding. When you remove one of your ideas from the table, you are paying attention to others. When you recast something you have said to make it more precise, you are listening to yourself and making improvements in your communication with others.

In terms of verbal behavior, noticing others' words and matching your language to them is a way of responding to important data (Garmston & Wellman, 1999). If a group member uses an appropriate metaphor, picking up that metaphor in your own speech validates the other person and builds group rapport. Consider this example: A group member describes a project as a "wild roller-coaster ride." You continue this metaphor in the group discussion with references to "peaks and valleys," "breakneck speed," "gasping for breath," and other related references, as appropriate. (Exercise some restraint so that the metaphor doesn't lose its power.) This technique helps to build group cohesiveness.

A more subtle approach is to match auditory words with other auditory words, visual with visual, and kinesthetic with kinesthetic. For example, a group member talks about hearing a number of "discordant" ideas being expressed. You respond by saying that you will try to "orchestrate" the discussion by identifying underlying themes you think you have heard. Your auditory word matches the other person's auditory word. This technique validates differences in learning styles.

▨ Reflection

Here are some statements that contain metaphors. Read each one and decide how you might respond to the person making the statement by using or building on the metaphor used:

- "I feel that all we're doing is running around putting out fires."

- "That old building is sucking the life right out of us."

- "Managing information systems is like going over Niagara Falls in a barrel."

In this next set of examples, determine whether each item has an auditory, visual, or kinesthetic image, and match your response to the same type of image.

- "How would you like to orchestrate our presentation to senior management?"

- "This project requires more assembly than I think we can handle."

- "Can you sketch out for me what the new plan will cover?"

▨ Notes

_____

_____

_____

_____

_____

◾ DAY 8: Group Norm #5– Paying Attention to Self and Others, Nonverbal Communication

The time to stop talking is when the other person nods his or her head affirmatively but says nothing.

—Anonymous

◾ Paying Attention to Self and Others, Nonverbal Communication

Because nonverbal communication—as exhibited in posture, gestures, voice tone and inflection, facial expression, proximity, and posture, for example—often carries more of the message than the words, being able to decode it is extremely important (Garmston & Wellman, 1999). That includes knowing what messages your own nonverbal behavior communicates and being able to read the nonverbal behavior of others. Remember that in instances of a mixed message—the words say one thing, but the nonverbal behavior says something else—the nonverbal is usually the stronger message and the one that is most clearly received by others

So, how might you get more in touch with your own and others' nonverbal messages?

Let's say that you notice that when Group Member A introduced an idea, Group Member B stopped participating. She moved her chair back from the table, got her calendar out, flipped through pages, and made notes. She seemed to have disengaged from the discussion. You know her behavior changed, but you don't know why. Because total group involvement is central to your task, you want to find out what is happening and pull her back in if she has indeed left. That is an example of paying attention to nonverbal cues.

Note that in the situation above, you have not made any conclusions about Group Member B's behavior. You have just observed a change. You have avoided what Chris Argyris (1986) calls *the ladder of inference*. In the ladder of inference, a common human pathway, we select data, add meanings, make assumptions, and draw conclusions that often lead to incorrect beliefs and actions.

Assume that you had started up the ladder. Here is what might have happened. You thought you saw Group Member B look at Group Member A when he spoke. You thought the look was strange and concluded that there was something going on between them. Then, you speculated about what that could be. You ended up concluding that Group Member B had found Group Member A's suggestion offensive and was upset with him. Note that you made all of this up. Your conclusion was not based on actual accurate data that you had verified. All of this took place in your own head so quickly that you were probably not aware of the rapid ascension. And no one observed this mental manipulation except you.

Climbing the ladder of inference too quickly is a very common human activity and one to guard against in observing group behavior. Notice behavior, but don't draw conclusions before checking out and confirming your data.

▩ Reflection

Observing Nonverbal Behavior. In the next meeting you attend, pay close attention to your nonverbal behavior. Are you sitting or standing? Where have you positioned yourself within the group? What is your facial expression? What is your posture? Do you have any particular mannerisms (propping up your head with your hand, playing with your hair or a piece of jewelry, twirling a pencil or pen)? If someone were to walk by, what message would your nonverbal behavior convey? Is it the message you want to send?

If you are comfortable doing so, ask a trusted colleague, who is also in the meeting, to give you some feedback. See whether his or her perceptions are similar to yours or whether they are different. After comparing data, is there anything you would like to change about how you communicate nonverbally?

Avoiding Climbing the Ladder of Inference. Here are some instances that can easily trigger an ascent up the ladder of inference. What alternative explanations might account for the following behaviors?

- A group member yawns a lot and occasionally closes his eyes.
- Two group members refuse to attend a breakfast meeting.
- One group member rarely makes a contribution unless asked. Her ideas are usually excellent.
- One group member consistently arrives 10 minutes after you start the meeting.

How can you find out what is really going on?

▩ Notes

_____

_____

_____

▧ DAY 9: Group Norm #6– Presuming Positive Intentions

Men willingly believe what they wish to be true.

—Caesar

▧ Presuming Positive Intentions

We serve ourselves and our group by assuming that others intend the best and are speaking and acting out of positive motives (Garmston & Wellman, 1999). If that is the case, then framing paraphrases and probes with this assumption in mind is likely to keep the group on a positive note and move the interaction forward.

By assuming positive intentions, we reduce threats, challenges, and defensiveness. We also keep emotions on an even keel by not responding immediately when something bothers us. When we hear something that could be taken in a negative way, it is best to take a deep breath and pause, and then make an assumption of positive intentions. A deep breath and a pause can lead to reframing that is based on the assumption of positive intentions.

In presuming positive intentions, we ask questions in the spirit of inquiry rather than the spirit of interrogation. We also actively solicit different views and interpretations.

▧ Reflection

Activity 1.

Here are the same situations given for Norm #5, with different instructions this time. Assume that each person is a professional who is committed to the welfare and success of your group. Using the alternative realities you generated for the reflection in Norm #5, along with this assumption, pose a question to each person about his or her behavior that is not threatening, less likely to produce defensive behavior, and helps you clarify intentions. We use the first instance as an example:

- A group member yawns a lot and occasionally closes his eyes. A presuming-positive-intentions response is this: "You seem tired. Have you recovered from that hectic schedule we kept last week?" A presuming-negative-intentions response: "Is this too boring for you? Don't let us keep you up."

- Two group members refuse to attend a breakfast meeting.

- One group member rarely makes a contribution unless asked. Her ideas are usually excellent.
- Another group member consistently arrives 10 minutes late.

Activity 2.

Here are some statements that contain presuppositions. Identify each one:

- If the other team had done what it was supposed to, they wouldn't be having this problem right now.
- We're done with brainstorming. Now, let's go back and identify the good ideas.
- Our previous leader should have cleared that for us before leaving.
- If the agenda had been set up properly, we wouldn't be running over.
- The books didn't arrive. Someone needs to call and let those people know what we think of them. They promised they would be here in 10 days.

▨ Notes

_____

_____

_____

_____

_____

_____

_____

▨ DAY 10: Group Norm #7–Pursuing a Balance Between Advocacy and Inquiry

Don't listen to what people are saying. Listen to why they are saying it.

—Anonymous

▨ Pursuing a Balance Between Advocacy and Inquiry

Advocacy is attempting to influence others. *Inquiry* is gathering more information about options. Balancing the two involves spending as much time and effort on inquiry as is spent on advocacy. This balance is essential for individuals as well as for the group. This norm is the last because it requires the other six to achieve this balance (Garmston & Wellman, 1999; Senge, Roberts, Ross, Smith, & Kleiner, 1994).

Balancing advocacy and inquiry accomplishes the following (Garmston & Wellman, 1998, pp. 46-47):

- Respects the rights of an individual to join the dialogue or remain silent

- Keeps track of the relationship between advocacy and inquiry that is occurring within the group

- Presents reasons for holding a position you advocate and how you arrived at it

- Inquires of others regarding their reasons for holding a position and how they arrive at it

One is just as necessary as the other. It is a question of balance and timing.

▨ Reflection

Activity 1.

Here are some pairs of partial statements of advocacy in which you are attempting to make your thinking and reasoning more apparent. In each pair, select the one that best fits the spirit of advocacy:

"These are the data that led me to believe . . ." *or*
"I believe very strongly that we should . . ."

"This is what is going on." *or*
"From the perspective of an outsider, here is what I see."

"I've thought about this a long time before making up my mind" *or*
"I've given this a lot of thought but only from my perspective. Do any of you see that I've missed something?"

"There is one part of this I don't feel I've thought through very well. Can one of you help me better define the problem?" *or*
"If anything is true, it's that I do understand what is going on."

Activity 2.

Here are some partial statements of inquiry in which you are asking others to make their thinking visible in a nonthreatening way. Again, choose the statement that is more likely to produce the answer you seek:

"For the life of me, I can't understand why you think . . ." *or*
"It would help me a great deal if you could explain your thinking about . . ."

"I think our underlying assumptions might be different. Would you be willing to tell us what you see as the 'givens' in this situation?" *or*
"Our underlying assumptions must be different. I think the group agreed that these are the ones we're dealing with."

"You haven't said much, Harry. You're so good at reframing problems that I'd like to know how . . ." *or*
"You haven't said a word, Harry. I don't have the slightest idea what you're thinking or feeling at this point. Are you for or against us?"

"I think our proposed solution may go against the values and beliefs of some group members. I'd like for each of us to talk about how the solution does or doesn't support our values and beliefs." *or*
"This proposed solution may go up against some people's values and beliefs. If that's the case, so be it. They'll have to learn to adjust."

▨ Notes

_____

_____

_____

_____

▨ DAY 11: Dialogue Versus Discussion

*As scarce as truth is, the supply has always been
in excess of the demand.*

—Josh Billings

Not only are there more effective patterns of talk (as exemplified by the seven norms), there are also different types of talking, often with different purposes. These different ways are presented in Figure 4.1.

In this schema, conversation is informal talking in which group members simply exchange information, ideas, thoughts, or feelings with each other, often with no purpose other than to enjoy the experience. At some juncture, the nature of the conversation may begin to change. If it starts to take on a more conscious, deeper purpose, it has reached a choice point. Group members decide consciously or unconsciously whether the talk goes into either dialogue or discussion.

Dialogue and discussion are two very different ways of talking, each with its own specific purpose and rules.

Dialogue is reflective learning in which group members seek to understand each others' viewpoints and assumptions by talking together to deepen their collective understanding. Dialogue often opens up the possibility of a better solution. The goal is finding common ground.

Figure 4.1. Ways of Talking

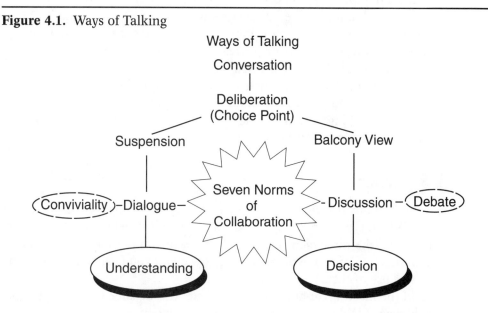

SOURCE: Garmston, R. J., & Wellman, B. M. Copyright © 1999. *The adopted school: A sourcebook for developing collaborative groups* (p.52). Norwood, MA: Christopher-Gordon. Reprinted with permission.

With dialogue, there is inquiry to learn and a desire to discover and unfold shared meaning, to integrate multiple perspectives, and to uncover and examine underlying assumptions. An appropriate discussion topic for dialogue might be the purpose and role of professional development in an organization.

The purpose of *discussion,* on the other hand, is to decide something. Discussion eliminates some suggestions from a wider field, with the stronger ideas taking precedence. In discussion, there is normally an action outcome. Most organizational meetings involve some form of structured discussion. There is a purpose and an anticipated outcome that moves the organization forward. In discussion, there is telling, selling, persuading, gaining agreement on one meaning or course of action, evaluating choices and selecting the best, and justifying and defending assumptions.

How one engages in dialogue and discussion has an effect on the group's productivity. In the schema above, conviviality is dialogue that focuses on comfort rather than real learning. Debate is discussion that relies on intimidation and intonation more than logic and reason. Neither fosters group growth and development or productivity.

According to Garmston and Wellman,

At its most ineffective, discussion is a hurling of ideas at one another. Often it takes the form of serial sharing and serial advocacy. Participants attempt to reach decisions through a variety of voting or consensus techniques. When discussion is unskilled and dialogue is absent, decisions are often of poor quality, represent the opinions of the most vocal members or the leader, lack group commitment, and do not stay made. Skilled discussions take place when there is (a) clarity about decision-making processes and authority, (b) knowledge of the boundaries surrounding the topics open to the group's decision-making authority, and (c) standards for orderly decision-making meetings. (1999, p. 57)

▨ Reflection

Think about organization meetings you've been involved in or led recently. Which type of talk happened? Was the talk largely structured discussions? Were the three elements of skilled discussion outlined above (clarity, boundaries, and order) in place? If not, how could you facilitate the development and use of them?

Did the meetings at any time degenerate into debate? Did they incorporate dialogue? Did dialogue ever slip into conviviality?

Was the type of talk appropriate for the purpose of each meeting? If not, why not? What could you have done to promote the type of interaction that best suited the purpose and desired outcome of the meetings?

▨ Notes

_____

_____

_____

_____

_____

_____

_____

_____

_____

_____

▨ DAY 12: Dialogue as Reflective Learning Process

He who differs from us, does not always contradict us;
he has one view of an object, and we have another,
each describes what he sees with equal fidelity, and
each regulates his steps by his own eyes.

—Samuel Johnson

Dialogue—what makes it different?

Recall what dialogue is: a reflective learning process in which people seek to understand each other's viewpoints and deeply held assumptions by talking together to deepen their collective understanding. The goal is increased understanding—not a decision, not a next step, just greater understanding on every person's part.

The basic internal skill in dialogue is suspending judgment. It means being open to what is happening in the moment and to what others are thinking and feeling. Suspending judgment also involves surfacing assumptions and beliefs, which influence our perceptions of reality.

According to Garmston and Wellman (1999),

> Dialogue creates an emotional and cognitive safety zone in which ideas flow for examination without judgment. Although many of the capabilities and tools of dialogue and skilled discussion are the same, their core intentions are quite different. Much of the work in dialogue is done internally by each participant as he or she reflects and suspends. (p. 55)

The value of greater understanding is that it is the basis for conflict resolution, consensus, and community building. If certain group members feel they have not been heard, they can sabotage a decision. Dialogue ensures that every person is heard and, ideally, understood. "Working from a foundation of shared understanding, group members can more easily and rationally resolve differences, generate options, and make wise choices when they move to the discussion side of the journey" (Garmston & Wellman, 1998, p. 56). The seven group norms are extremely important for establishing effective dialogue.

▨ Reflection

The reason this contemplation focuses on dialogue rather than structured discussion is that most of us are more experienced in the latter. It may be our primary style. We are skilled and comfortable. And that is important because effective discussion is a critical skill for group members. However, so is dialogue, but most of us are not as skilled and comfortable with this form of talking. Consider the following questions:

- How readily do members of your group engage in dialogue?

- How do you encourage people to share assumptions and their thinking on issues with the purpose of shared understanding?

Think of a problem or issue you are facing that you would like to ask your group to dialogue about.

- How will you teach them to dialogue?

- How will you structure the meeting?

How can you establish a culture in which your colleagues are skilled and willing to use dialogue to develop more shared meaning?

▨ Notes

_____

_____

_____

_____

_____

_____

_____

PART II
Key Aspects of Effective Group Functioning

From research and best practice, we know how effective groups function. Talking to each other appropriately is one way, but there are others. The contemplations in Part II focus on some key aspects of how effective groups function: structuring a solid foundation, setting norms, building an agenda, attending to logistics, and creating an appropriate environment.

Other contemplations explore how to make decisions, handle conflict, and avoid bias and stereotyping. The next set deals with recalcitrant group members, encouraging participation, giving and receiving feedback, and solving problems of group functioning. The final set focuses on leaders getting off to a good start with their groups, the leader's role in solving group problems, and evaluating a group's stage of development.

▧ DAY 13: Sources of Group Energy

We are what we repeatedly do.
Excellence, then, is not an art, but a habit.

—Aristotle

How do effective groups establish a solid foundation for functioning?

They structure themselves so that they draw energy from five sources. These sources, or values, according to Garmston and Wellman (1999), are efficacy, flexibility, craftsmanship, consciousness, and interdependence. "These values are founded in a belief that human energy is inexhaustible when five energy sources for high performance are accessed and developed" (p. 70). Adherence to these values results in an inexhaustible source of energy, energy that is self-perpetuating. The group both feeds and draws from these energy sources.

Here are brief descriptions of the five values (Garmston & Wellman, 1999):

Efficacy is the assurance that an individual or a group has the capacity to take effective action and is willing and able to do so. "Efficacious groups regard events as opportunities for learning, are motivated by and committed to achieving shared goals, learn from experiences, focus resources where they will make the greatest difference, know what they know and do not know, and develop strategies to learn what is needed" (p. 173).

Flexibility refers to a group's ability to view situations from a variety of different perspectives. "Groups who develop this energy source honor and value diversity within and outside the group, attend to both rational and intuitive ways of thinking, can collectively shift perspective, and utilize a wide array of thinking and process skills" (pp. 173-174).

Craftsmanship is taking pride in one's work and continuously striving to improve performance. "Groups accessing this resource invest energy in honing and inventing better ways to do their work, honor in themselves and others the arduous journey from novice to expert, manage time effectively, and continually improve inter- and intragroup communications" (p. 174).

Consciousness is being aware of one's internal experience: thoughts, feelings, behaviors, motivations, and their effects on others. "Groups using this energy source maintain awareness of their values, norms, and identity; monitor congruence of espoused beliefs and behaved beliefs; and stand outside themselves to reflect on its processes and products" (p. 175).

Interdependence is a recognition of the linkages between people, institutions, communities, cultures, and all aspects of human existence. "Interdependent groups value and trust the process of dialogue, have awareness of their multiple relationships and identities with other groups, and regard disagreement as a source of learning and transformation" (p. 175).

▧ Reflection

Think about a group you have responsibility for. On a scale of 1 (low) to 10 (high), rate your group on these five energy sources:

Efficacy

1   2   3   4   5   6   7   8   9   10

Flexibility

1   2   3   4   5   6   7   8   9   10

Craftsmanship

1   2   3   4   5   6   7   8   9   10

Consciousness

1   2   3   4   5   6   7   8   9   10

Interdependence

1   2   3   4   5   6   7   8   9   10

If your group falls below a 7 on any source, you may want to assist group members in strengthening their commitments. According to Garmston and Wellman (1998, p. 23), you can do that as follows:

- Teach the group about the different energy sources: what they are, what they offer, what different manifestations look like, and how they access the energy source.

- Structure the environment to support the energy source or sources. For example, perhaps the group is weak on craftsmanship. Exposing group members to a set of best practices in an area of its work can help raise quality performance.

- Work with the group to help them improve. You might sit in with a group to raise key points and ask pertinent questions when aspects of the group's functioning related to craftsmanship arise. You would use many of the norms of collaboration in your role as mediator (see Days 5-10).

- Collect data on the energy source (efficiency, flexibility, craftsmanship, consciousness, or interdependence) being considered and reflect on what the data tell the group about its functioning and how it might improve.

Which interventions are most appropriate for your group? How will you carry out your chosen strategy?

▨ Notes

▨ DAY 14: Establishing Clear Roles and Functions

The best leader is the one about whom,
after the group has finished, someone says,
"Who was the leader?"

—Lao Tze

To operate effectively and efficiently, groups need to be clear about their roles and functions. It is the group leader's responsibility to make sure clarity exists about (a) how the group was formed, (b) which people participate and why, (c) the charge of the group, (d) how the charge relates to the organization's overall mission and vision, (e) what resources the group has at its disposal, (d) the time frame, (f) reporting responsibilities, and (g) how the group decides to go about its work.

Groups that are clear on all these factors are much more inclined to tap into one of their energy sources: efficacy. Members are more likely to believe that their group has the capacity to act and is willing and able to do so. The leader considers the parameters of the work, conveys them to the group, and answers any questions or resolves any issues that might be in the way (or works with group members to address unresolved issues).

One important step is for the leader and the group to set guidelines for how the group will go about its work. Here are some items on which the group should agree:

Logistics
- Meeting dates, times, and locations
- Structure of meetings (e.g., agenda, time designations for items, distribution of written documents prior to the meeting, etc.)
- How to keep and disseminate records of the group's work
- Whether there will be refreshments and, if so, how they will be provided

How the group functions
- Roles for group members (e.g., convener, recorder, facilitator, or reflector)
- Processes for decision making
- Guidelines for handling conflict
- How to handle issues of confidentiality and any conflict of interests
- Limits of legal and/or fiduciary responsibility, if applicable
- Basic conversational courtesies: listening to each other, not interrupting, being respectful of each other, and carrying on one conversation at a time (see norms for how people talk with one another in groups, Day 2)
- Guidelines for giving and receiving feedback

- Honoring spontaneous humor and fun as the group works
- Determining how the guidelines will be adhered to or enforced

How individuals function
- Using "I" statements when speaking for oneself (except in paraphrasing)
- Notifying the convener (or other designated person) when unable to attend a meeting
- Being on time for meetings and staying for the entire meeting
- Responding to voice mail and e-mail messages within a reasonable length of time
- Agreeing to do what each member commits to doing or renegotiating the task with the group
- Agreeing to turn off cell phones during meetings

Although most of these items should be decided by the group itself, the leader sets a tone for how he or she wants the group to function by requesting that the group set ground rules and that members follow them. Again, this is an important step in building efficacy.

If a group doesn't set its own guidelines, certain patterns of behavior will emerge anyway from the dynamics of the group. The problem with "default" behavior patterns is that they may not be the ones you want. Changing existing patterns is always more difficult than beginning with a slate of established ground rules. Moreover, if you as leader don't establish guidelines, you will lose influence and later find yourself dealing with problems that could have been avoided. You are also responsible for following the guidelines yourself. If you don't, group members may see that as license to ignore one or more guidelines.

Establishing these operational guidelines in a group is very common. What is rarely done, however, is to agree on how the norms will be enforced. All too often, established guidelines are ignored because there is no guideline set for enforcing the agreed-upon behavior. Members may feel uncomfortable pointing out inappropriate behavior, so that very quickly in the life of a group, the guidelines may be negated or followed only when members find it convenient or easy.

As a leader, you can make a valuable contribution to your group by insisting on a process for ensuring that members follow the guidelines. This might entail giving each person explicit permission to alert his or her peers to infractions and clarifying the expectation that they do so—that is part of being an effective group member. In fact, in the early life of the group, you might want to practice intervening with members who violate the guidelines so your group will feel more comfortable enforcing the norms. Here is a place where the skills of giving and receiving feedback (see Days 27 and 28) become very important.

▩ Reflection

Consider the following scenario: As a midlevel administrator, you have just been designated chair of the curriculum committee. The previous leader is out on medical leave for an indefinite period. This is a relatively new group whose charge is to make recommendations on how to strengthen the curriculum. The group's members represent various departments and schools within your district. They meet once every three weeks.

The first time you join the group for its regularly scheduled meeting, you notice several things that raise your concerns. Only 7 of the 13 members come to the meeting. One person missing is the assistant superintendent of curriculum, your immediate supervisor—the person who appointed you to this position. Of the other members who are not present, 4 are teachers.

The curriculum committee's vice-chair arrives five minutes late and has a conversation with one group member before starting the meeting. The topic for the day is further explanation of the extent to which the district's elementary science curriculum meets state and national standards. The district's science coordinator makes a presentation on alignment, with student achievement data for the science portion of the statewide test. During the presentation (which is very well done), you notice that two committee members leave to run errands, one walks into a corner to answer his cell phone, and another appears to fall asleep.

After the presentation, the vice-chair leads the group through a problem identification exercise to identify possible factors contributing to a decline in the student achievement at the sixth-grade level. At this point, all members are in attendance and participating, so much so that they often interrupt each other. Sometimes, two or more people talk at the same time.

The group decides to follow up on this session with some small-group work to prepare to generate possible solutions to the problem. However, because the meeting ran past the allotted time, some people left without getting their assignments. The vice-chair asked remaining members to contact those who had gone and give them their assignments.

The group adjourned a half-hour later than scheduled and set the next meeting day with just three people present.

As the new leader, what would you do to increase the efficiency and effectiveness of this group? The following questions may help you in your thinking:

- This group appears not to have set any guidelines for its own behavior or apparently isn't following any that they may have made. Which ones do you think would help them function better?

- Do you see any possible problems in the composition of the group? How would you deal with the absences?

- How do you integrate yourself into this group, especially with the vice-chair?

- What behaviors do you think you should model?
- Your first exposure to this group was at its regular meeting. What might have been different had you first met with the vice-chair and two or three members?

▨ Notes

▨ DAY 15: Structuring an Effective Meeting

Ask any group of managers in any country in the world to list
their three most time-consuming activities. Invariably, "meetings"
will appear among the three. I have asked this question of more
than 200 groups, and in every case but 3, more than three-
quarters of each group indicated that half their time spent in
meetings is wasted. The problem . . . is not being sure which half.

—Alec R. MacKenzie

Ask Alec MacKenzie's question, and you will get the same answer: unnecessary meetings, meetings that accomplish nothing, or meetings that go on and on. There is no inherent value in a meeting for the sake of a meeting. Every meeting needs to have a purpose, anticipated outcomes, and an effective process that involves all members.

Good group meetings just don't happen; they are the result of careful planning and leadership. One key is building a workable agenda and following it (Mundry, Britton, Raizen, & Loucks-Horsley, 2000; Scholtes, Joiner, & Streibel, 1999).

Here are some suggestions on structuring an effective meeting:

- Have a clear purpose for the meeting.

- Build an agenda around the purpose. Gather input from group members about the agenda. Others may want to add, delete, or reorder an item.

- Determine (a) which items are information items for which discussion is appropriate and (b) which are action items that should result in a clearly defined next step, and (c) label the items as appropriate.

- Decide how much time to allot to each item and indicate that on the agenda. You can negotiate more time if necessary, but at least you have a proposed plan for staying on schedule.

- Describe the process to be used for each item, including the domain of talk and the decision-making strategy (e.g., majority preference) for the action items. Each topic on the agenda needs to have a process associated with it so members know how to approach the item.

- Place controversial topics at or near the beginning of the agenda. Placing such topics at the beginning of the meeting ensures that the group will have sufficient energy to address the topic.

- Distribute the agenda prior to the meeting. Group members need to have sufficient time to review an agenda and prepare for the meeting. They may want to gather data, read certain articles, or prepare a presentation.

- Before starting the meeting, review the agenda with group members to see whether there are any suggestions for changes. Incorporate changes as appropriate and then begin the meeting.

- Stick to your agenda unless the group decides to renegotiate items or time. Often, issues will emerge that a group had not predicted, and an agenda will need to be modified.

- Have someone take notes. Depending on the purpose of your meeting, you may need detailed minutes. In most instances, a page of action notes is sufficient—a listing of the next steps decided on and who is responsible for what. These serve as a record of the meeting and should be distributed to group members and others who need to know about your group's work.

- Conclude with a check to assess how effective your meeting was. Each group member could complete the following stems: "What I liked best about our meeting is . . . ," "What I wish we could have done differently is . . . ," or "What I still feel unresolved about is. . . ."

▨ Reflection

Sketch out a tentative agenda for an upcoming meeting. Distinguish between information items and action items. Assign times to each item as well as a process. Put any controversial items up front. Decide who will take notes and what type of notes you want. Send out the agenda beforehand.

At the end of your meeting, ask for feedback. What did people like and not like about the "new" agenda?

▨ Notes

_____

_____

_____

_____

▨ DAY 16: Providing Logistical Supports

Success is the sum of the details.

—Harvey S. Firestone

Good logistics won't save a poorly designed meeting, but a well-planned event or activity can be ruined by poor logistics.

Planning meeting logistics is beyond the scope of this book. There are many excellent resources available, including *Designing Successful Professional Meetings and Conferences in Education* (Mundry et al., 2000) and *The Team Handbook* (Scholtes et al., 1999). However, several aspects of logistics directly affect any group's ability to do its work and are important to review.

As a leader, you need to make sure that the following have been addressed to support your group:

Provide group members with complete premeeting information in a timely manner. Your event can get off to a shaky start if members have not been informed about time, place, parking, agenda, and other logistical aspects of the meeting. Informing your members enables them to come prepared to do the group's work.

Select a room that is appropriate for the group's work. Not any vacant room will do. The room needs to accommodate the work the group is doing. That includes the configuration of space, access to natural light, the positioning of the table and chairs, and the acoustics (see Day 17).

Provide appropriate materials for the group's work. These may include audiovisual aids; computers; charting materials; and prepared reference materials, handouts, or worksheets. Print materials need to be error free and look professional. There must be adequate space on the walls for putting up posters or flip chart sheets to help the group track its work.

Arrange for refreshments. Groups can work more effectively if they have ready access to food and drink for the duration of their event. Unless you start a meeting right after a meal, it is a good idea to have food and drink available at the beginning of a meeting rather than halfway through or at the end.

Plan the agenda so that members can make a transition into the meeting. People often come into a meeting with the day's events—rather than the meeting—primary in their minds. They may be thinking about a conflict they are having, the report they are working on, or getting to a meeting after this one. If you structure a transition activity at the beginning, you will help members focus on the immediate situation. One way of doing that is to pose the question, "What is foremost in your mind right now that you want to put on hold for the next two hours, and what are your expectations for this meeting?" Having each person respond can make the transition, and you can then proceed with your agenda.

▒ Reflection

Think about your next meeting coming up. Have all these logistical supports been provided for? If not, what do you need to attend to? What moves can you make as the facilitator to better ensure that group members participate fully?

▒ Notes

_____

_____

_____

_____

_____

_____

_____

_____

_____

▨ DAY 17: Setting Up the Meeting Room

When facilities are proper, they go unnoticed.
—Marion E. Haynes

What do you do when company comes to visit? Clean the house? Make sure the guest room is ready? Make a trip to the grocery? Ask the kids to put their toys away?

These are typical ways in which we prepare to welcome our guests and make them comfortable. But how many of us do this for our meetings? It is what David Perkins (1992) calls defining the *surround*. The surround is comprised of the features that influence thought and action in a group. These may be psychological, emotional, cognitive, or physical in nature. As a group leader, you have some influence on all of these, but you have the most control over the physical features of the meeting room.

What is important to know about the physical features? Here are some points to remember (Garmston & Wellman, 1999):

Everyone should be able to see and hear each other. There are many different seating arrangements for groups of all sizes: semicircle, horseshoe shape, and so on. Depending on the acoustics, a group of 40 or more may require amplification.

Every participant should be able to see the group leader and the flip chart, screen, or other visual aids. Seeing visual aids and the facilitator is essential for the group to proceed with the work. Participants should face away from the door or entryways. (See below for some suggestions for the group leader to orchestrate the meeting.)

The chairs and tables (if used) should be appropriate for the size of the group. Extra tables and chairs that are not used disturb the energy balance in the room and should be removed. Taking out empty chairs allows for a more direct group connection.

The arrangement of the room should allow for individual movement and for subgroupings; participants need to see the whole room as their space rather than restrict themselves to a particular chair. People have a tendency to select the same seat in meetings. Changing seats produces more energy in the room and gives participants a different perspective.

Tools for helping the group with its work (e.g., flip charts, white boards, or other recording devices) should document the group's work. Certain tasks such as planning, problem solving, and decision making require access to data as well as charting materials. Being able to post written materials on the wall and write on flip charts or the wall is critical to a group's work.

In setting up the room, provide different areas where the facilitator can be strategically positioned to lead the group. For example, one of the facilitator's jobs is to give instructions, and that can best be done by communicating in three different mediums: space, voice, and language. In giving directions, the facilitator selects a key spot, uses a credible voice that elicits support, and gives the directions. Then, he or she moves to a different place and checks for understanding, using a softer, more approachable voice. The facilitator has now established a physical space in which he or she can change roles, from checking in with group members to correcting and clarifying behaviors (Garmston & Wellman, 1999).

▨ Reflection

Activity 1.

Think of a recent meeting that you attended. Recall the room arrangement. Did it satisfy the following criteria? Did it . . .

- Allow participants to see each other?
- Enable participants to see the facilitator and any visual aids?
- Seat nonparticipants separately from participants?
- Match the chairs to the number of participants?
- Have sufficient room for people to move around?
- Have adequate tools to support the meeting?

If there was something amiss, what could you do to correct it for the next meeting?

Activity 2.

Recall the last time you gave directions to a group. How did you do so? If you followed Garmston and Wellman's suggestion, what would you do differently?

▨ Notes

_____

_____

_____

_____

▨ DAY 18: Group Decision Making

*When making a decision of minor importance, I have found it
advantageous to consider all the pros and cons. In vital matters,
however, such as the choice of a mate or profession, the decision
should come from the unconscious, from somewhere within
ourselves.*

—Sigmund Freud

Many groups get stuck because they are not sure how to make a decision.

There are many ways a group can go about its decision making. Actually,
the way a group makes a decision may depend on the nature of the decision to
be made. Not all decisions require the same amount or base of support. Some
need a lot; others need much less.

Here are five major ways that a group may make a decision:

- By full consensus

- By "sufficient consensus" (see Day 19)

- By a majority vote

- By delegating the decision to a subgroup

- By delegating the decision to an individual group member

For any of these decision-making options, the full decision may lie with
the group or some part of the group, or the group may solicit input from
nongroup members, such as other staff members, administrators, or stakeholders.

Generally, the more a decision requires commitment to any kind of collective action, the more broadly based the decision needs to be.

▨ Reflection

Here are some decisions that a group might be making. Using the approaches listed above, how should each be made? Recognize that the approach you use may well depend on the context, and that may generate alternative approaches:

- Set a date for the next group meeting.

- Select a new group leader.

- Determine the focus of the next professional development program.

- Recommend a new curriculum.

- Decide what color and type of folders to use in the next professional
  development activity.

Think about the groups you are currently leading. Are the members in each of them clear about how they make decisions? Do they make decisions in different ways, depending on the level of commitment needed? If your answer to either question is no, what can you do to strengthen their abilities to use appropriate decision-making processes?

▩ Notes

_____

_____

_____

_____

_____

_____

_____

_____

_____

_____

▨ DAY 19: Reaching Consensus

Minds are like parachutes; they work best when open.

—Lord Thomas Dewar

Groups often talk about wanting consensus, but consensus is very hard to achieve, and in many instances, it is simply not necessary. Some decisions don't require that broad a base of support. Some groups are not constituted in a way that makes consensus possible. In other instances, they may not have the time or resources to push for a full consensus.

For most groups, what Garmston and Wellman (1999) call *sufficient consensus* is enough. Sufficient consensus means that at least 80 percent of the group agrees and are prepared to act. The remaining 20 percent may not concur, but they have agreed not to sabotage the action. They are not in agreement, but they can live with the decision—whatever it may be.

However, if full consensus is required of a group, Garmston and Wellman (1999, pp. 58-59) provide a list of conditions that need to be present before a full consensus is possible:

1. There should be clarity about the group's purpose and how it operates.

2. Power in the group needs to be distributed equally. Consensus doesn't work in hierarchical groups.

3. The group needs to have the autonomy to choose consensus. A group may find it difficult to reach full consensus if it is getting pressured to make a decision and move on.

4. Consensus requires a great deal of time and patience, which a group may not have.

5. Group members must be willing to spend time examining their own functioning.

6. Individual group members must be willing to reflect on their own thinking and be open to change.

7. Group members and the group as a whole must continually sharpen communication, participation, and facilitation skills.

▨ Reflection

Given this list of the requirements for effective consensus building and the caveat of sufficient consensus, think of the groups you lead.

Are any structured for consensus building? If so, which ones? How do you know? What types of decisions might they be making in which a full consensus is necessary? For what types of decisions would a sufficient consensus be more appropriate? As a group leader, how do you establish the structures and conditions within a group for consensus building?

Here is a reminder: Effective groups don't always use consensus; their decisions depend on the situation. More consensus building is not always necessary or even desirable.

▨ Notes

_____

_____

_____

_____

_____

_____

_____

_____

_____

_____

DAY 20: Dealing With Conflict

Conflict can be seen as a gift of energy, in which neither side loses and a new dance is created.

—Thomas Crum

Learn to love conflict! Yeah, sure. You must be kidding. Why should I learn to love conflict? Conflict is nothing but trouble.

Many of us have been conditioned to avoid conflict or become skillful in minimizing its impact. But there is a cost in doing so. Conflict that is suppressed or avoided tends to reappear. It often takes the form of passive-aggressive behavior in which a person appears to go along with a decision but then sabotages it. Avoiding conflict also lessens the chances that all alternatives will be explored and the most effective decision made.

Here are several common ways in which groups deal with conflict (Scholtes et al., 1999, pp. 7.4-7.5). All except one (possibly two) fail to resolve the issue:

Avoid the conflict. Some people believe there is no value in attempting to bring conflict out in the open and resolve it. They may also be fearful of the consequences; therefore, they will attempt to avoid the conflict.

Smooth it over. If the conflict can't be avoided, the next best strategy, according to the conflict avoiders, is to minimize the conflict so that relationships remain intact. There is an attempt to assuage individuals and move on. The real issues are never dealt with and are likely to resurface.

Force the conflict. This strategy attempts to overpower group members to get them to accept a certain position. Personal relationships are disregarded; achieving the goal is more important. This is a competitive, win/lose approach that may backfire when the conflict reemerges.

Compromise. In a compromise, the different sides each give up something for the greater good. Compromising is tricky. Sometimes it works; sometimes it doesn't. It can be either a lose/lose or a win/win strategy, depending on how much the different sides have to give up.

Problem solve. Face the conflict head on and work through it. This strategy is the one that retains both personal goals and group relationships. It is most likely to produce a win/win outcome for all concerned. It does, however, require skill to be successful. Problem solving draws heavily on the norms of how people in groups talk to one another.

Your approach to group conflict is a choice you make.

▨ Reflection

Think of situations in which groups you have been part of have encountered conflict. Which of the above approaches did your group take? With what results?

Which of the above approaches is the one you naturally gravitate to? As a leader, one of your greatest gifts to your groups is your ability to face conflict directly and work through it. If you are not comfortable using problem solving in a conflict situation, what can you do to strengthen your confidence and comfort level and encourage the same in your group members?

▨ Notes

_____

_____

_____

_____

_____

_____

_____

_____

▨ DAY 21: Conflict as Opportunity

*The question is not how to eliminate conflict but how
to capitalize on its constructive aspects.*

—Marion E. Haynes

A prerequisite to facing conflict directly and working through it is having a mind-set of conflict as an opportunity. Conflict is a chance to look at situations from a new perspective and perhaps generate an entirely new solution. That is what conflict can provide, especially when people demystify conflict.

According to Garmston and Wellman (1999), conflict is nothing more than energy moving through a system. The meaning that people bring to conflict produces the conflict. And that meaning comes from one's own background, along with the culture of the group. Just as group members perceive reality through their own lenses, they also see conflict in highly individualized ways.

A useful distinction can be made between affective conflict and cognitive conflict. *Affective conflict* is interpersonal conflict. It is Harry and Jane versus Ralph and Denita, or the primary versus the intermediate team. This type of conflict deters group functioning. It contributes to decreased commitment, less cohesiveness, decreased empathy, and decisions that do not produce the desired results.

Cognitive conflict is a disagreement over ideas and approaches. It is a difference of opinion about, for example, how teachers should handle students' misconceptions in a constructivist approach to teaching and learning. This type of conflict is characteristic of a high-performance group. It separates the ideas from the people and holds the ideas up for close examination. It leads to greater commitment, increased cohesiveness, heightened empathy, deeper understanding, and decisions that produce the desired results.

Thus, one significant goal of an effective group is to increase cognitive conflict and reduce affective conflict.

▨ Reflection

Think about a group you have led that experienced some conflict. Was the conflict more affective or cognitive? How do you know? What happened? How was the conflict resolved—or was it?

How can you help a group avoid affective conflict and stay within the realm of cognitive conflict?

▨ Notes

▨ DAY 22: Don't Shoot the Messenger

Hey, don't get mad at me. I'm only the messenger.

—Any of us at some time in our past

How does the bearer of bad news avoid being directly associated with the bad news?

A series of specific steps called "How Not to Get Shot" (HNTGS) is Michael Grinder's (1998) strategy for allowing your audience to disassociate you from the bad news that you deliver. The purpose of HNTGS is to create a space and time for a group to grapple with difficult issues and still preserve professional relationships. In her book, *Leadership and the New Science* (1992), Margaret Wheatley stresses the association between energy and relationships and how solutions emerge from the relationships among people.

Here is a description of each of the HNTGS steps:

1. *Go visual.* Information delivered orally makes the group dependent on the person delivering the information. If someone does not hear it, the information will need to be repeated. Information displayed visually on a flip chart allows group members to look at it as they choose and process it in their own time frame. In other words, having a visual display makes the participants less dependent on the messenger.

2. *Get it off to the side.* The messenger can facilitate communication by separating issues from solutions and creating situations in which group members can grapple with difficult issues and still maintain relationships. Once the information is displayed visually, "get it off to the side" to create a "third point." The messenger and group can then focus on this additional point in examining the issues rather than having "two-point" communication, directly between the leader and the group members.

3. *Redirect the group's attention.* Because group members follow the messenger's eyes, use this to redirect their attention to the visual message. For example, place a "frozen hand" gesture toward the group and then move the hand toward the visual message. At the same time, the messenger should turn his or her head and eyes in coordination with the hand gesture. When the group looks at the visual message, the messenger can then look at the group to read people's nonverbal reactions. This sets the stage for the messenger to be proactive in facilitating a group toward its desired outcomes.

4. *In speaking, avoid possessive modifiers.* Instead of saying, "my report" or "my schedule," talk about "the report" or "the schedule." Neutral modifiers decrease defensiveness and the attribution of blame. This helps to maintain relationships.

5. *Separate the location of the problem from the location of the solution.* This suggestion is predicated on the idea that locations have memory—whether positive or negative. For example, do you remember where you were when President Kennedy was assassinated or when the attack on the World Trade Center and the Pentagon occurred? Using separate locations allows the messenger to use third point to the issue and second point to the group for solutions. The result is a situation that preserves relationships by creating a location for issues and a separate location for the solutions.

6. *Use an approachable voice.* The messenger chooses voice tone very carefully and deliberately. In sending information and talking about the issue, use a credible voice. When talking with people, seeking information, and identifying solutions, use an approachable voice.

7. *Use specific descriptions.* Specific language adds to the quality of communication because there is less left ambiguous. Clarity of intent and clarity of description are important facets to understanding issues. Being specific is key to clarifying issues and ensuring common understanding.

8. *Position the body at 90 degrees.* This allows the speaker to point to the location of the visually displayed issue while pivoting and gesturing to the group. Ninety degrees is a natural placement to create the third point. "Once the third point is created, then the rest of the components of How Not To Get Shot fall into place better" (p. 33).

▨ Reflection

Think of a time when you had to deliver unwanted news or when you were in the audience receiving unwanted news. How was it delivered? Where was the messenger delivering the news? What nonverbal communication did he or she use in delivering the news? What happened in the group after the news was delivered?

Imagine a situation in the future when you may deliver a message that people really don't want to hear. How would you use each of the steps mentioned above? What will you say, and how will you use your nonverbal communication to support your words? How might you expect the outcome to be different?

▨ Notes

▨ DAY 23: Resolving Conflict

The doors we open and close each day decide the lives we lead.

—Flora Whittemore

As a leader, you have a responsibility to model conflict resolution directly. However, although you may be skillful in doing so, you may be dealing with other people who are not as skilled.

If emotions rise to the surface and interaction becomes heated, keeping yourself under control is a basic survival skill. It takes a high level of emotional maturity and some highly developed skills not to get sucked into the maelstrom of conflict. Here are some suggestions for remaining under control (Garmston & Wellman, 1999; Scholtes et al., 1999):

- Breathe deeply. Take a deep breath or two or three before saying a word. Under stress, our breathing becomes shallow, and oxygen is not distributed as well throughout our bodies.

- Remember that the behavior of others is rarely malicious or evil in intent. Most people are motivated by positive intentions (see Day 9).

- Feel the energy of the conflict and move toward it rather than away. Often in the midst of conflict, we want to retreat, to physically leave the premises, or at least to put some psychological distance between ourselves and the conflict. We are in a better position to dispel the conflict by moving toward and embracing it—physically and psychologically.

- Know that the behavior of the people involved in the conflict is rarely planned, thought out, or calculated. In most instances, conflict arises out of events, not deliberation.

- Conflict may stem from events, but it is not born out of the moment. All conflicts have some history (e.g., a previous conflict or negative experience).

- Use paraphrasing. Remember that paraphrasing shows the other person that you value his or her thoughts, feelings, and positions. It also helps you keep the focus off yourself and on the other person.

- Try to keep the conflict cognitive in nature rather than affective. Separate the issues from the people who are connected to them.

- If you feel yourself "losing it," take a time-out at least for yourself and perhaps for the entire group. Get a drink of water, make a trip to the restroom, or go outside for some fresh air.

▨ Reflection

In reviewing this list of suggestions, which ones do you use and feel comfortable with? Which ones might you try?

As a leader of groups, how can you help other group members use these techniques for themselves?

▨ Notes

_____

_____

_____

_____

_____

_____

_____

_____

_____

_____

▧ DAY 24: Impact of Bias and Stereotyping

*In the great blooming, buzzing confusion of the outer world we
pick out what our culture has already defined for us, and we tend
to perceive that which we have picked out in the form stereotyped
for us by our culture.*

—Walter Lippman

Any instances of bias and stereotyping in a group negatively affect group consciousness (one of the energy sources) and can hinder the functioning of the group. Bias and stereotyping are violations of the norm of paying attention to self and others.

There are six primary sources of bias and stereotyping in work groups. Each one and its impact are discussed briefly below:

1. *Excluding minorities or women from group membership.* It is important to have your group membership reflect your stakeholders or constituency. A nonrepresentative group can raise questions among the larger community that can hinder the group's efficacy (one of the energy sources). For example, a question might be, "Why is that group making decisions about Black History Month with just one African American represented?" Similar issues that surface within the group ("Why are there no women here?") can also negatively affect efficacy.

2. *Expecting a member of a minority group or a woman to speak for his or her race, ethnic group, or gender.* Often when individuals are a minority in a group, other group members will expect them to know and expound on, for example, the Native American point of view, the female perspective, or what Hispanics are likely to believe.

There are two fallacies here: one is that a racial or ethnic group has a unified perspective, which is rarely the case. There will almost always be a diversity of opinion. Second, even if there were a unified perspective, it would be inappropriate to expect an individual to know and espouse that view. It is fine to ask, "What would our various stakeholders think of this idea?" It is not appropriate to ask a member of a minority group for the opinion of that group as a whole.

3. *Expressing certain stereotypes or bias in assumptions made about group members.* Making any type of assumption about group members because of their race, ethnicity, or gender is another source of bias and stereotyping. Assumptions can be either positive or negative. For example, someone might say, "I bet you don't know the way to the Eastside recreation area. You live on the Westside, right?" Or "This is a good role for Jack. He can stack the chairs and move the tables before we leave. He's a big guy; he can handle it."

In such cases, you are, in essence, speaking for the person without the person validating what is correct and appropriate for himself or herself.

4. *Discounting another's contribution or attributing it to someone else.* A common occurrence in groups is discounting or ignoring someone's contribution only to affirm it when another person picks it up. Then, the idea is likely to be attributed to the second source rather than the first. There also is a good chance that the first contributor is perceived as a lower-status person and the second as a higher-status individual.

5. *Using jokes, puns, or other expressions of humor that reflect negatively on a particular group.* With the heightened awareness of diversity issues in recent years, this type of bias and stereotyping in groups appears to have lessened. However, it does still exist. Attempts to be funny using racial, ethnic, or sexual humor are more likely to be sources of embarrassment than sources of humor.

6. *Using derogatory language or offensive terms.* Referring to any group member using a derogatory or offensive term—publicly or privately—is simply crude and degrading. Moreover, it is likely to backfire. The news media have reported numerous stories about people who have lost their positions by making racial or sexual slurs.

The presence of any bias or stereotyping in a group usually indicates that the norm of paying attention to oneself and others is not being followed. Group members who don't realize the impact of their behavior on others can affect the group's efficacy and perhaps even the outcome of its work.

▨ Reflection

Here is an opportunity to practice. What follows are several statements reflecting bias and stereotyping made in a group. Imagine yourself leading the group: How would you handle the situation?

- "I'm sure that Leslie won't be able to meet on Saturday. I bet she has to take care of her kids."

- "I heard the best dumb blonde joke the other day. These two blondes were walking down the street. . . ."

- "Lester speaks Spanish, too. The two of you should talk."

- "What is the Puerto Rican take on this situation?"

How can you, as leader, heighten group members' awareness of the negative effects of bias and stereotyping?

▨ Notes

▨ DAY 25: Dealing With Disruptive People

I couldn't believe what William did. Without saying a word to our trainers or to any of us in the group, he brought in a portable TV and turned on the basketball game just as our session was starting.

—A workshop participant

As long as there are groups, there will be people in them who exhibit difficult behavior. Often, these individuals don't want to be in the group in the first place.

As a leader, you cannot allow the inappropriate behavior of a few people to control the group. There are constructive techniques for dealing with a person who is disruptive because he or she doesn't want to be part of the group:

If people don't want to be in your group, confirm their sentiments rather than trying to convince them of the advantages of their participation. There may be individuals who prefer to be some place other than in your group, especially when participation is required. The best way to diffuse these people is to simply accept their feelings: "You're saying that you don't want to be here and that attendance creates a hardship for you. I'm not in a position, however, to do anything about that. Perhaps you should speak with. . . ." Another possible response might go something like, "Yes, I know you resent the compulsory attendance policy. I hope you'll find something today that will be useful. If you have any specific questions or concerns, please see me at break." People will often drop their hostility once they have expressed their negative feelings, especially if you respond with a paraphrase.

Deal directly with the person privately. If you chose the one-on-one approach, take the person aside. Try to determine the source of the person's behavior. Does he or she not want to be part of the group? If not, why not? Is it best for this person to leave? If he or she stays, what can mitigate the inappropriate group behavior? Does this person need anything from you or the group? If so, can you and/or the group provide the necessary support?

Instead of dealing directly with a recalcitrant person, allow group pressure to emerge. Sometimes, approaching people directly is not the best strategy. Having group members deal with difficult individuals as peers may be much more effective. Members will often do this on their own; you need not do anything. If not, at some point you may want to turn to the group to ask members how they feel about something the difficult person has said or done. If the situation is best handled privately, you may want to ask one or two group members to speak to the person at the first opportune moment.

Set up circumstances that allow people who should not be there to exit gracefully. If participation in the group is voluntary, a person may realize that he or she doesn't belong and leave. This can occur naturally when the group is establishing itself: clarifying purpose, adopting norms of behavior, assigning roles, and outlining tasks to be completed. An individual may see that participation just isn't appropriate or possible and withdraw from the group.

Whatever strategy you choose for people who don't want to be there, use it promptly. By doing so, you establish the group as a safe place to work. Your actions show that you will not allow one or two people to disrupt the group's progress.

▧ Reflection

Consider this situation: You are coinstructor of a six-week professional development series for elementary and middle school teachers. The focus is on incorporating algebraic concepts in the K-7 mathematics curriculum. The goal is to better prepare students for taking algebra in grade eight, which is now a required class unless students are specifically exempted.

There are 30 teachers signed up for the program, 2 from each elementary and middle school in your district. Most teachers volunteered to participate in the series; a few were appointed by their principals.

At the first meeting, you notice two people who act as if they don't want to be there. They fidget in their seats, read the newspaper, and occasionally just get up and leave for a short period. One is an elementary teacher; the other, a middle school teacher. You learn during the introductions that each was appointed by her principal to attend. During their introductions, you attempt to humor them, but they don't laugh.

As the day progresses, they continue their behavior. What do you do?

▧ Notes

_____

_____

_____

_____

_____

▨ DAY 26: Eliciting Participation From Everyone

*An atmosphere of free exchange can be created only when
participants see that a mutual sharing of opinions
and ideas is welcome.*
—Marion E. Haynes

In virtually every group, there are those who want to talk a great deal and those who say little. Ideally, you want to hear from everyone. As a leader, you may need to reign in those people who tend to talk too much and set up structures to encourage those more reticent to express themselves.

Remember one of the basic tenets of communication: Silence doesn't mean agreement or consent. Unless people talk, it is hard for you to know what they are thinking and feeling. There are numerous ways to draw out people who say little in a group. Here are a few suggestions:

- Provide opportunities for group members to write their ideas and pair with another to share their responses, as well as speak in the large group. Some may be more willing to share a response after they have had the opportunity to write it down and say it aloud to one person.

- In brainstorming, have participants first write down one or more idea or suggestion. Go around the room, having each person contribute one item aloud. After all contributions have been written down, have another period of writing. Keep this up until you have a sufficient number of responses for your task.

- Set up smaller groups of two to four, in which conversation may come easier for those who dislike speaking in a larger group.

- Extend your wait time so those who need time to think can do so before speaking.

You may also need to be proactive to make sure that some people do not dominate the conversation. For example:

- Establish a group norm about each member having his or her fair share of airtime. (This tends to keep the talkers under control more than it gets the reticent ones to speak up.)

- Say "Let's hear from someone who hasn't spoken" before giving a frequent speaker the floor.

- If all else fails, take the person aside at a break and discuss the importance of hearing from each person and not having one or two dominate the discussion. In extreme cases, you may have to set a rule such as only one comment per fifteen-minute period.

Following these suggestions will earn you the respect of the group and only occasionally, the hostility of one or two people who seem unable to control the urge to talk at every opportunity. It will contribute to group bonding—you with the group and group members with one another—and will help establish your group as a safe place to work. You will also be helping people monitor their own participation.

▩ Reflection

By the end of the first session of your six-week professional development series for elementary and middle school teachers, you see that you have a number of very extraverted people. Six people speak frequently, and about the same number haven't said a word beyond their introductions. Two of the outspoken teachers are from the same school, one whose test scores are the highest of any elementary school in the district.

One of your activities was a brainstorming session in which the teachers were asked to generate a list of all the algebraic concepts they thought were appropriate for students to learn at the primary, intermediate, and middle school levels. During this activity, you noticed that some teachers participated very little.

At the end, you asked for a voice vote on moving the time of the next session up half an hour. A majority said yes, so you adjusted the time.

What participation problems do you see? What steps can you take to balance participation? How can you make sure that you know what your more reticent members are thinking and feeling? How can you avoid making "majority rule" decisions that affect each member of the group?

▩ Notes

▨ DAY 27: Giving Negative Feedback

The two words "information" and "communication" are often used interchangeably, but they signify quite different things. Information is "giving out;" communication is "getting through."

—Sydney J. Harris

Effective groups are skilled at giving and receiving feedback. This is one way in which groups learn and are able to make course corrections. Feedback is absolutely essential if individuals and their groups and organization are to grow and develop. In fact, exchanging feedback should become part of an organization's culture. Giving and receiving feedback should be as common as getting a new assignment. It is simply part of how a group or an organization functions.

What follows are some ground rules for giving and receiving negative feedback. Why only negative? Because giving positive feedback is easy. Most people welcome positive feedback. The negative is trickier.

▨ Giving Feedback

The Context. Negative feedback should be accompanied by feedback on what is going well. There is a tendency to provide feedback only when there is a problem, thus making the feedback largely negative. Knowing what they are doing well is as important for people as knowing what they need to improve on.

The timing of feedback is critical, as well as the circumstances under which it is delivered. It is normally not a good idea to give negative feedback by e-mail or voice mail. The nonverbal communication channel is largely absent, and your message can easily be misconstrued. Also, the person may receive the message at an inappropriate time.

Also, avoid giving negative feedback when you or the other person is feeling strong emotions or when either of you is experiencing low self-esteem. Don't give feedback when the other person is leaving, can't do anything to correct the problem, or when the physical setting is inappropriate. Avoid "gotchas" that focus on all the things the person has done wrong. Make sure your feedback is on target and useful to the other person.

The Delivery. Always speak first for yourself—not for other people—even if you know others feel the same way. Describe the behavior as objectively as possible, without using labels. Don't exaggerate or be judgmental. Keep your feedback to the facts you know firsthand. Help people hear and accept your compliments. In the midst of your negative feedback, they may not focus on the positives you convey.

The Sequence. Here are six key stems for you to complete in delivering constructive feedback:

- "When you . . ."
- "I feel . . ."
- "Because I . . ."

Provide a time-out for the other person to respond to what you have said. Then continue with:

- "I would like . . ."
- "Because . . ."
- "What do you think?"

Provide another opportunity for the person to react. Here is an example: "When you come to group meetings without your assignments completed, I feel let down and angry. It keeps us from getting our work done in a timely fashion. You are pulling us off our time schedule. (Pause for discussion.) I would like you to have your work done at the beginning of each meeting. That way, we're much more likely to adhere to our time frame. What do you think?"

▨ Reflection

Think of a team member to whom you would like to give some feedback about his or her behavior. Write that feedback in the space below.

Now, go back and review it against the criteria listed above. To what degree does your feedback follow the guidelines? What changes will you make?

▨ Notes

_____

_____

_____

DAY 28: Receiving Negative Feedback

People love to talk but hate to listen. Listening is not merely not talking. . . . It means taking a vigorous, human interest in what is being told to us. You can listen like a blank wall or like a splendid auditorium where every sound comes back fuller and richer.

—Alice Duer Miller

This contemplation is a continuation of Day 27, which discusses giving feedback.

Receiving Feedback

The Context. You are likely to find yourself receiving feedback from someone who may not be skilled in following the rules discussed above. If that is the case, you may be able to help the deliverer recast the feedback so it corresponds more closely to those rules. If that doesn't work, you may simply have to listen to what the person has to say and work your way through.

Here are some suggestions to help you receive feedback (Scholtes et al., 1999):

First and foremost, breathe. When you are hearing things you may not want to hear, it is normal to tense and tighten your muscles and start breathing shallowly. Try to take deep breaths so your brain gets sufficient oxygen. Listen carefully, without interrupting, to what the person has to say. Ask for clarity or for specific examples.

After the other person has made his or her major point, paraphrase the message to acknowledge the speaker and to make sure you have heard correctly. At this point, you are just checking for understanding. Next, agree with whatever the person has said that is true. This may require suppressing your ego and its normal defensive reaction. For example, agree to the fact that you failed to notify three important people about a meeting, if that is what you did.

If you didn't do what your colleague says you did, speak up—again, in a nondefensive manner. Say something such as, "I understand that you think I failed to notify those three people about the meeting. I see it differently. Here is my understanding of what happened. . . ."

Don't rush into resolution unless the desired solution is readily apparent. Perhaps an apology is in order. If so, you can apologize, identify what you are apologizing for, and state what you will or won't do as resolution. Or perhaps you need time to think something over. If so, tell your colleague that you need some time and when you will get back to him or her.

▨ Reflection

Think back to a recent time someone gave you negative feedback. How did you respond? Were you able to listen? Were you able to admit that you acted inappropriately, if that was the case? Did you feel yourself getting defensive? If so, how did you know? What were the clues? Was the situation resolved? If so, how? What could you have done differently?

As a leader, how can you help your group members understand and follow the rules for giving and receiving feedback?

▨ Notes

_____

_____

_____

_____

_____

_____

_____

_____

_____

▨ DAY 29: Presentation Skills

The key to successful leadership today is influence, not authority.

—Kenneth Blanchard

As a group leader (facilitator, presenter, coach, or consultant), your ability to influence others lies in how you present and conduct yourself, what you say, and what position you hold in the group and in your organization. Your most powerful source of influence is always how you present and conduct yourself; your behavior always speaks louder than your words. And your words have more ability to influence than your position of authority.

How long does it take to size up new group leaders? Probably just a few seconds after they speak a few words. Or judgment can be made simply by observing them for a few minutes before the meeting starts. On the basis of this initial impression, many group participants develop an opinion (positive or negative) about a leader. This opinion may change over time, but if it is negative, the leader must work harder to turn the image around.

What can you do early in a session to help strengthen your image in a group? Here are some suggestions:

Greet and call group members by name. To be recognized and called by name is a basic human need. Show your understanding of this by arriving at a meeting in time to greet people individually and call them by name. If you know them, you may also want to talk with each person briefly or make a comment that is relevant to each. If you don't know the people, introducing yourself before the meeting starts and learning members' names will strengthen your credibility. Following this suggestion will help you make a connection with the group and show that you value and respect each person.

Start with a strong opening. Think about various meetings you have attended over the years, speeches people have made, or sermons you have heard in church—especially their beginnings. How many do you recall? How do most people start? Here are some examples of opening statements. Which do you see as strong? Weak? Why?

"Albert Einstein said, 'I never teach my pupils, I only attempt to provide the conditions in which they can learn.'"

"I really appreciate you giving up your Saturday morning to be with us."

"We want to start by introducing . . . and thanking the people who made today possible."

"I start by offering you a guarantee! By the time this session is over, you'll be able to . . . But if you can't, I'll refund. . . ."

The ability to come up with a strong beginning is a real skill and one that anyone leading a group can develop with practice.

Get your participants speaking to each other or to you and the group as a whole after you make your opening comments. The most powerful opening is one in which you make a few strong opening comments to establish both scope and tone for the meeting; then, get your participants talking. The earlier all voices are heard in the room, the better participation you will have. They may be talking with each other, perhaps introducing themselves or discussing their expectations for the meeting; or they may be speaking to the entire group and to you as the leader. Whatever the topic, they do the talking, not you.

This is very important because it establishes a participative tone for the meeting: It lets group members know that you are not going to stand in front of them and lecture the whole time. How many times have you heard group leaders say, "I'm not going to do all the talking, so I'll need to hear from each one of you"—and then talk at you for the next hour? By that time, you have taken in all you are able to and have lost faith in your facilitator. By involving the members, you are treating the group in a respectful manner. Moreover, you can gain their credibility by adhering to your word and making the session meaningful and relevant to them.

Eliminate tics from your speech or any annoying mannerisms. Over the years, many people pick up "speech tics." These are superfluous words or sounds that work their way into our speech and become patterned responses. Can you spot the tics in the sentences below?

"Well, let me tell you about what happened in my organization."

"Let me tell—I want to tell—yes, I'll tell you about what happened."

"Uh, I want to tell you, uh, about what happened, uh, in my organization."

"You know, in my organization, the most wonderful thing happened. It was so unusual—you know—something that has never happened before."

We are often unaware of our tics, how often we use them, or how disruptive they are. Sometimes, listeners will be so distracted by the tic that they tune out the message. We may also have acquired some annoying mannerisms. Perhaps we look at one side of the room more than the other, use a pencil or pen in a distracting way, or stand in an awkward position. Just like the speech tics, these can detract from the positive impression we want to make on our group and more important, from the content of the presentation.

Conclude with a strong ending. Think of various endings you have heard in speeches. Can you label the endings as either strong or weak? What made an ending strong? Here are some examples of concluding statements. Which do you see as strong? Weak? Why?

"Thanks so much for coming. This was a good session. We'll meet again in two weeks. Don't forget to send me an e-mail if you have any questions."

"I want to thank each of you today for your hard work. Roger, your intervention got us unstuck. Dale, Margaret, and Jennifer, each of you moved our work forward."

"I want to close with a short poem I wrote last night about our charge."

"Here are three cartoons that capture the essence of our work. Note in the first. . . ."

▨ Reflection

Consider asking someone (ideally a colleague) to give you feedback on how you present yourself to a group. That includes your overall presence, how you meet and greet people, whether you have any tics in your speech or annoying mannerisms, and how you begin and end the meeting. If your colleague finds anything that needs improvement, monitor your own behavior closely. Then, ask for more feedback to see how you have improved.

▨ Notes

_____

_____

_____

_____

_____

_____

_____

_____

_____

▨ DAY 30: Handling Problems

Leadership has a harder job to do than just choose sides.
It must bring sides together.

—Jesse Jackson

It is inevitable. Some groups will experience problems, such as a breakdown in communication, members that do not perform adequately, and misunderstandings about the work they are responsible for completing. It will be your responsibility to give them some help. What will you do? Here are some options (Scholtes et al., 1999, pp. 7.7–7.10):

If possible, anticipate and prevent the problem in the first place. Although it is not always possible, many problems can be averted if a group has been formed properly and takes time up front to prepare to function as a team. For example, a group should make sure that it has the right mix of people, is clear about its purpose, and has sufficient resources. Members should take time to get to know each other and establish a set of norms for group behavior. If a group that you are responsible for hasn't taken these first steps, you are likely to encounter problems sooner or later.

Let the group deal with the problem. Think of any problem as belonging to the group rather than to individuals. When a group has difficulties functioning, the source usually lies within the system rather than with individual group members. The group as a whole is often doing something that has let the problem develop or exacerbate. Therefore, it should be the group's responsibility to resolve it. If at all possible, help the members solve it for themselves.

Intervene if you think it necessary to get the group back on task. Sometimes, the group can't solve the problem itself, and you will need to intervene. That intervention may be minimal or more extensive, depending on the nature of the problem.

Talk to some group members privately. Either give them feedback about their own behavior or suggestions as to what they can do in the group.

Another option is to meet with the group. You might simply observe its functioning and provide feedback. Or you may need to play a more assertive or confrontational role to help the group deal with its problem.

A strategy of last resort is to restructure the team by removing some people and/or adding others. This approach, unfortunately, can tarnish a team's image and inhibit its functioning even though the team member or members are gone.

▨ Reflection

Think for a moment of a group you were responsible for that had a problem. Was it a problem that could have been prevented? Did the group solve the problem itself? Did you have to intervene? What was the end result? What would you do differently the next time one of your groups encounters a problem?

▨ Notes

_____

_____

_____

_____

_____

_____

_____

_____

_____

_____

▧ DAY 31: Six Domains of Group Development

*Good, better, best; never let it rest till your good is better
and your better is best.*

—Anonymous

So, once a group, always a group. Is this right?

Although the configuration may remain the same, group dynamics evolve. All groups attempt to balance getting the work done with attending to process, creating ongoing tension.

Six domains influence how effectively a group functions (Garmston & Wellman, 1999). For success in each domain, group members need to have domain-specific knowledge, skills, and structures. What follows is a brief explanation of each domain, its underlying assumptions, and what is necessary for the group to function effectively in that domain.

Getting Work Done. Group members understand that tension between task and process is ongoing and believe that it and the group's work are manageable. Key knowledge includes being able to function in modes of both dialogue and discussion, knowing how to conduct successful meetings, being able to facilitate groups, and skill in designing efficient and effective meetings.

Doing the Right Work. The underlying assumption here is that vision, mission, and values focus group energy and help ensure that they are doing the right work. Members need to know how to live with conflict, work with problems that seem unmanageable, increase their adaptivity, and create a sense of community.

Working Interdependently. The key underlying assumption for this domain is that diversity is an asset and subgroups must work together and see each other as valuable resources. They must adhere to the seven norms of collaboration. They must also be proficient in discussion and dialogue, meeting management, facilitating groups, and living with conflict.

Managing Systems. Knowing when to reject linearity and think more systemically and systematically as the tasks become more complex is the underlying assumption. Key knowledge includes living with conflict, handling unmanageable problems, being adaptive, and creating community.

Developing Groups. Regardless of its current productivity, a group can always be more effective and/or more efficient. Adapting to change is a task for both individuals and groups. The underlying assumption is that both individual and group orientations are required to plan and implement significant change. The requisite knowledge includes information on these six domains, living with conflict, valuing community, and the principles for creating community.

Adapting to Change. The underlying assumption here is that if groups are to be effective, they must constantly adapt to external environments. The more unstable the environment, the more the group must maintain an outward orientation. Required knowledge includes working with conflict, adapting to change, and creating community.

It is easy to see how interrelated these six domains are. For example, skill in dialogue and discussion are essential for two of the six. Being effective at dialogue requires internalization of the norms of collaboration. These are also prerequisites for dealing with conflict.

▨ Reflection

It is helpful to assess a group's stages of development in these six domains. Garmston and Wellman (1999, p. 161) suggest a five-point scale set up on the continuum shown in Table 4.1.

Think of a group that you are part of. Assess your group on each one of the domains shown in Table 4.2 (Garmston & Wellman, 1999, p. 161).

What do you see your group doing well? Where could it function better? What knowledge and skills does it need that it doesn't have? What can you do to move your group forward?

Table 4.1 Assessing the Six Domains of Development

Domain	1	2	3	4	5
Getting work done					
Doing the right work					
Working interdependently					
Managing systems					
Developing your group					
Adapting to change					

SOURCE: Garmston, R. J., & and Wellman, B. M. Copyright © 1999. *The adaptive school: A source book for developing collaborative groups.* Norwood, MA: Christopher-Gordon. Reprinted with permission.

Table 4.2 Stages of Development

Stage of Development	Descriptor
1. Beginning	Unconscious incompetence (don't know what they don't know)
2. Emerging	Unconscious incompetence and conscious competence
3. Developing	Conscious competence
4. Integrating	Conscious competence and unconscious competence
5. Innovating	Unconscious competence

SOURCE: Garmston and Wellman (1999, p. 161).

References

Argyris, C. (1986). Skill incompetence. *Harvard Business Review, 64*(5). (*Harvard Business Review* Reprint #86501)

Garmston, R. J., & Wellman, B. M. (1998). *The adaptive school: Developing and facilitating collaborative groups*. El Dorado Hills, CA: Four Hats Seminars.

Garmston, R. J., & Wellman, B. M. (1999). *The adaptive school: A sourcebook for developing collaborative groups*. Norwood, MA: Christopher-Gordon.

Grinder, M. (1998). *Patterns of permission: The science of group dynamics*. Battleground, WA: Michael Grinder & Associates.

Haynes, M. E. (1998). *Effective meeting skills*. Menlo Park, CA: Crisp Publications.

Mundry, S., Britton, E., Raizen, S., & Loucks-Horsley, S. (2000). *Professional meetings and conferences in education: Designing, planning, and evaluating*. Thousand Oaks, CA: Corwin.

Palmer, L. J. (1998). *The courage to teach: Exploring the inner landscapes of a teacher's life*. San Francisco: Jossey-Bass.

Perkins, D. (1992). *Smart schools*. New York: Free Press.

Scholtes, P. R., Joiner, B. L., & Streibel, B. J. (1999). *The team handbook*. Madison, WI: Oriel.

Senge, P. M., Roberts, C., Ross, R. B., Smith, B. J., & Kleiner, A. (1994). *The fifth discipline fieldbook*. New York: Doubleday.

Wheatley, M. J. (1992). *Leadership and the new science*. San Francisco: Berrett-Koehler.

CORWIN
PRESS

The Corwin Press logo—a raven striding across an open book—represents the happy union of courage and learning. We are a professional-level publisher of books and journals for K-12 educators, and we are committed to creating and providing resources that embody these qualities. Corwin's motto is "Success for All Learners."